Turkish
Phrase Book
&
Dictionary

Berlitz Publishing
New York   Munich   Singapore

Contacting the Editors
Every effort has been made to provide accurate information in this publication, but changes are inevitable. The publisher cannot be responsible for any resulting loss, inconvenience or injury. We would appreciate it if readers would call our attention to any errors or outdated information. We also welcome your suggestions; if you come across a relevant expression not in our phrase book, please contact us: Berlitz Publishing, 193 Morris Avenue, Springfield, NJ 07081, USA. Email: comments@berlitzbooks.com

All Rights Reserved
© 2008 Berlitz Publishing/APA Publications GmbH & Co. Verlag KG, Singapore Branch, Singapore

Berlitz Trademark Reg. U.S. Patent Office and other countries. Marca Registrada. Used under license from Berlitz Investment Corporation.

First Printing: May 2008
Printed in Singapore

Publishing Director: Sheryl Olinsky Borg
Project Manager: Farida Aslanova
Translation: Ali Osman Tezcan
Revision: Ared Misirliyan
Cover Design: Claudia Petrilli
Interior Design: Derrick Lim, Juergen Bartz
Production Manager: Elizabeth Gaynor
Cover Photo: © Masterfile
Interior Photos: p. 12 © Studio Fourteen/Brand X Pictures/age fotostock; p. 17 © Baloncici, 2007 Used under license from Shutterstock, Inc.; p. 24 © Eric Sweet; p. 38 © Roman Krochuk, 2006/Shutterstock, Inc.; p. 48 © Corbis/fotosearch.com; p. 51 © Purestock/Alamy; p. 56 © Quendi Language Services; p. 60 © Eric Sweet; p. 73 © Quendi Language Services; p. 80 © Eric Sweet; p. 85 © Netfalls, 2007 Used under license from Shutterstock, Inc.; p. 96 © Eric Sweet; p. 101 © Imageshop.com; p. 105 © image100/Corbis; p. 108, 111 © Eric Sweet; p. 115 © 2007 Jupiterimages Corporation; p. 124 © Eric Sweet; p. 133 © 2007 Jupiterimages Corporation; p. 141 © Jupiterimages/Brand X/Corbis; p. 142 © Stockbyte/Fotosearch.com; p. 145 © Corbis/2006 Jupiterimages Corporation; p. 149, 151 © Eric Sweet; p. 160, 171 © 2007 Jupiterimages Corporation; inside back cover © H.W.A.C.

Contents

Survival

Food

People

Fun

Special Needs

Resources

Dictionary

Pronunciation

This section is designed to familiarize you with the sounds of
Turkish using our simplified phonetic transcription. You'll find the
pronunciation of the Turkish letters explained below, together with
their "imitated" equivalents. To use this system, found throughout the
phrase book, simply read the pronunciation as if it were English, noting
any special rules below.

Letters underlined in the transcriptions should be read with slightly
more stress than the others, but don't overdo this as Turkish is not
a heavily stressed language.

Consonants

Letter	Approximate Pronunciation	Symbol	Example	Pronunciation
c	like j in jam	j	**ceket**	jeh·<u>keht</u>
ç	like ch in church	ch	**kaç**	kahch
g	like g in ground	g	**gitmek**	geet·<u>mehk</u>
ğ	1. at the end of a word, it lengthens the preceding vowel		**dağ**	dah*
	2. a silent letter between vowels		**kağıt**	kah·<u>iht</u>
	3. after e, like y in yawn	y	**değer**	deh·<u>yehr</u>
h	like h in hit	h	**mahkeme**	mah·keh·<u>meh</u>
j	like s in pleasure	zh	**bagaj**	bah·<u>gahzh</u>
r	trilled r	r	**tren**	trehn

| s | like s in sit | s | **siyah** | see·<u>yahh</u> |
| ş | like sh in shut | sh | **şişe** | shee·<u>sheh</u> |

Letters b, d, f, k, l, m, n, p, t, v, y and z are pronounced as in English.

*Bold indicates a lengthening of the sound, an extra emphasis on the vowel sound.

Turkish consonants are typically shorter and harder-sounding than English consonants. When reading Turkish words, be sure to pronounce all the letters.

Vowels

Letter	Approximate Pronunciation	Symbol	Example	Pronunciation
a	like a in father	ah	**kara**	kah·<u>rah</u>
e	like e in net	eh	**sene**	seh·<u>neh</u>
ı	similar to i in ill	ih	**tatlı**	taht·<u>lih</u>
i	like ee in see	ee	**sim**	seem
o	like o in spot	oh	**otel**	oh·<u>tehl</u>
ö	similar to ur in fur	ur	**börek**	bur·<u>rehk</u>
u	like oo in cool	oo	**uzak**	oo·<u>zahk</u>
ü	like ew in few	yu	**üç**	yuch

Turkish vowels are quite different from English vowels. As with consonants, they are generally shorter and harder than English vowels. In the pronunciation guide, certain vowels are followed by an "h" to emphasize the shortness of the sound.

Diphthongs

Letters	Approximate Pronunciation	Symbol	Example	Pronunciation
ay	like ie in tie	ie	bay	bie
ey	like ay in day	ay	bey	bay
oy	like oy in boy	oy	koy	koy

i

Türkçe (Turkish) is the native language of the 70-some million inhabitants of the Republic of Turkey, and is spoken by large numbers of ethnic Turks living outside of Turkey. The Turkish alphabet used today dates only from 1928, when Atatürk, the founder of Modern Turkey, chose to replace the Ottoman script that had been used for centuries.

Turkish differs from English in two important ways. First, affixes take the place of many words that, in other languages, would be written separately (such as pronouns, negatives and prepositions); these affixes are attached to a base word. Second, it features "vowel harmony"; this restricts which vowels may appear within a word. So, while affixes in their standard forms have the vowel "i" or "e", this may change when the affix is attached to another word. For example, the suffix **in** (´s) stays **in** in **evin** (the house's), but becomes **un** in **memurun** (the official's) and **ün** in **gözün** (the eye's).

How to Use This Book

These are the most essential phrases in each section.

Sometimes you see two alternatives in italics, separated by a slash. Choose the one that's right for your situation.

Essential

A *one-way [single]/ round-trip [return]* ticket.	**Sadece *gidiş/ gidiş dönüş* bileti.** <u>sah</u>·deh·jeh gee·<u>deesh</u>/ gee·<u>deesh</u> dur·<u>nyush</u> bee·leh·<u>tee</u>
How much?	**Ne kadar?** <u>neh</u> kah·dahr
Are there any discounts?	**İndirim var mı?** een·dee·<u>reem</u> <u>vahr</u> mih

You May See...

PERONLARA	to the platforms
DANIŞMA	information
YER AYIRTMA	reservations

Train

Where *is/are*...?	**...nerede?** ...<u>neh</u>·reh·deh
– the ticket office	**– Bilet gişesi** bee·<u>leht</u> gee·sheh·see
– the information desk	**– Danışma masası** dah·nihsh·<u>mah</u> mah·sah·<u>sih</u>
– the luggage lockers	**– Bagaj dolapları** bah·<u>gahj</u> doh·lahp·lah·<u>rih</u>

Words you may see are shown in *You May See* boxes.

Any of the words or phrases preceded by dashes can be plugged into the sentence above.

10

Turkish phrases appear in red.

Read the simplified pronunciation as if it were English. For more on pronunciation, see page 7.

Ticketing

When's...to Istanbul?	**İstanbul'a...ne zaman?** ees·<u>tahn</u>·boo·lah... <u>neh</u> zah·mahn
– the (first) bus	– **(ilk) otobüs** (<u>eelk</u>) oh·toh·<u>byus</u>
– the (next) flight	– **(bundan sonraki) uçak** (boon·<u>dahn</u> sohn·rah·<u>kee</u>) oo·<u>chahk</u>
– the (last) train	– **(son) tren** (sohn) trehn
Where can I buy tickets?	**Nereden bilet alabilirim?** <u>neh</u>·reh·dehn bee·<u>leht</u> ah·lah·bee·<u>lee</u>·reem

▶ For numbers, see page 167.

The arrow indicates a cross reference where you'll find related phrases.

Information boxes contain relevant country, culture and language tips.

i Cash can be obtained from **paramatik** (ATMs), which are located throughout Turkey. Some debit cards and most major credit cards are accepted. Be sure you know your PIN and whether it is compatible with Turkish machines. ATMs offer good rates, though there may be some hidden fees.

You May Hear...

Lütfen, *biletiniz/pasaportunuz*. <u>lyut</u>·fehn bee·leh·tee·<u>neez</u>/pah·sah·por·too·<u>nooz</u>

Your *ticket/passport*, please.

Expressions you may hear are shown in *You May Hear* boxes.

Color-coded side bars identify each section of the book.

▼ Survival

Arrival and Departure

Essential

I'm here on *vacation [holiday]/ business*.

Tatil/ İş için buradayım. tah·<u>teel</u>/<u>eesh</u> ee·cheen <u>boo</u>·rah·dah·yihm

I'm going to...

...gidiyorum. ...gee·<u>dee</u>·yoh·room

I'm staying at the...Hotel.

...otelinde kalıyorum. ...oh·teh·leen·<u>deh</u> kah·<u>lih</u>·yoh·room

You May Hear...

Lütfen, *biletiniz/ pasaportunuz.* <u>lyut</u>·fehn bee·leh·tee·<u>neez</u>/pah·sah·pohr·too·<u>nooz</u>

Your *ticket/ passport* please.

Ziyaret sebebiniz nedir? zee·yah·<u>reht</u> seh·beh·bee·<u>neez</u> <u>neh</u>·deer

What's the purpose of your visit?

Nerede kalıyorsunuz? neh·reh·deh kah·<u>lih</u>·yohr·soo·nooz

Where are you staying?

Ne kadar kalacaksınız? <u>neh</u> kah·dahr kah·lah·<u>jak</u>·sih·nihz

How long are you staying?

Kiminlesiniz? kee·<u>meen</u>·leh·see·neez

Who are you with?

Passport Control and Customs

I'm just passing through.

Sadece geçiyorum. <u>sah</u>·deh·jeh geh·<u>chee</u>·yoh·room

I would like to declare...

...beyan etmek istiyorum. ...beh·<u>yahn</u> eht·mehk ees·<u>tee</u>·yoh·room

I have nothing to declare.

Beyan edeceğim birşey yok. beh·<u>yahn</u> eh·deh·jeh·<u>yeem</u> <u>beer</u> shay <u>yohk</u>

You May Hear...

Gümrüğe tabi eşyanız var mı? gyum·ryu·<u>yeh</u>
tah·<u>bee</u> ehsh·yah·<u>nihz</u> vahr mih

Do you have anything to declare?

Bunun için gümrük vergisi ödemeniz gerekir.
boo·<u>noon</u> ee·<u>cheen</u> gyum·<u>ryuk</u> vehr·gee·<u>see</u>
ur·deh·meh·<u>neez</u> geh·reh·<u>keer</u>

You must pay duty on this.

Lütfen şu çantayı açınız. <u>lyut</u>·fehn shoo
chahn·tah·<u>yih</u> ah·chih·nihz

Please open that bag.

You May See...

GÜMRÜK	customs
VERGİSİZ EŞYALAR	duty-free goods
BEYAN EDECEK EŞYASI OLANLAR	passengers with goods to declare
BEYAN EDECEK EŞYASI OLMAYANLAR	passengers with nothing to declare
PASAPORT KONTROLU	passport control
POLİS	police

Money and Banking

Essential

Where's...? · · · **...nerede?** ...<u>neh</u>·reh·deh

– the ATM · · · – **Paramatik** pah·rah·mah·<u>teek</u>

– the bank · · · – **Banka** bahn·<u>kah</u>

– the currency exchange office · · · – **Döviz bürosu** dur·<u>veez</u> byu·roh·soo

What time does the bank *open/close*?	**Banka saat kaçta *açılıyor/kapanıyor*?** <u>bahn</u>·kah sah·aht kach·<u>tah</u> ah·chih·<u>lih</u>·yohr/ kah·pah·<u>nih</u>·yohr
I'd like to change *dollars/pounds* into lira.	***Dolar/İngiliz Sterlini* bozdurmak istiyorum.** doh·<u>lahr</u>/een·gee·<u>leez</u> stehr·lee·<u>nee</u> bohz·door·<u>mahk</u> ees·<u>tee</u>·yoh·room
I want to cash some traveler's checks [cheques].	**Seyahat çekleri bozdurmak istiyorum.** seh·yah·<u>haht</u> chek·leh·<u>ree</u> bohz·door·<u>mahk</u> ees·<u>tee</u>·yoh·room

ATM, Bank and Currency Exchange

Can I exchange foreign currency here?	**Burada döviz bozdurabilir miyim?** <u>boo</u>·rah·dah dur·<u>veez</u> bohz·doo·rah·bee·<u>leer</u> mee·yeem
What's the exchange rate?	**Döviz kuru nedir?** dur·<u>veez</u> koo·<u>roo</u> neh·deer
How much is the fee?	**Ne kadar komisyon alıyorsunuz?** neh kah·dahr koh·mees·<u>yohn</u> ah·<u>lih</u>·yohr·soo·nooz
I've lost my traveler's checks [cheques].	**Seyahat çeklerimi kaybettim.** seh·yah·<u>haht</u> chehk·leh·ree·<u>mee</u> <u>kie</u>·beht·teem
My credit card was lost.	**Kredi kartım kayboldu.** <u>kreh</u>·dee kahr·<u>tihm</u> <u>kie</u>·bohl·doo
My credit cards have been stolen.	**Kredi kartlarım çalındı.** <u>kreh</u>·dee kahrt·lah·<u>rihm</u> chah·lihn·<u>dih</u>
My card doesn't work.	**Kartım çalışmıyor.** kahr·<u>tihm</u> chah·<u>lihsh</u>·mih·yohr

▶ For numbers, see page 169.

You May See...

KARTI TAK	insert card
İPTAL ET	cancel
SİL	clear
GİR	enter
PİN NUMARASI	PIN
ÇEKİLEN PARALAR	withdraw funds
CARİ HESAPTAN	from checking [current account]
TASARRUF HESABINDAN	from savings
FATURA	receipt

i

Banka (the bank) and **postahane** (the post office) are good options for exchanging currency. **Döviz bürosu** (currency exchange offices) are also located in many tourist centers, though if you decide to change money in an exchange office, look around for the best rate and keep your eye on the commission. Also, remember to bring your passport, in case you are asked for identification.

You May See...

The monetary unit is the **Yeni Türk Lirasi**, abbreviated **YTL**. One **YTL** is divided into one hundred **yeni kuruş**, abbreviated **YKr**.
Coins: 1, 5, 10, 25, 50 **YKr** and 1 **YTL**
Notes: 5, 10, 20, 50 and 100 **YTL**

Transportation

Essential

How do I get to town?	**Şehire nasıl gidebilirim?** sheh·hee·<u>reh</u> <u>nah</u>·sıhl gee·deh·bee·<u>lee</u>·reem
Where's...?	**...nerede?** ...<u>neh</u>·reh·deh
– the airport	– **Havaalanı** hah·<u>vah</u>·ah·lah·nıh
– the train [railway] station	– **Tren garı** <u>trehn</u> gah·<u>rih</u>
– the bus station	– **Otobüs garajı** oh·toh·<u>byus</u> gah·rah·<u>jih</u>
– the subway [underground] station	– **Metro istasyonu** <u>meht</u>·roh ees·tahs·yoh·<u>noo</u>
How far is it?	**Ne kadar uzakta?** <u>neh</u> kah·dahr oo·zahk·<u>tah</u>

Where can I buy tickets?	**Nereden bilet alabilirim?** neh·reh·dehn bee·leht ah·lah·bee·lee·reem
A *one-way [single]/ round-trip [return]* ticket.	**Sadece *gidiş/ gidiş dönüş* bileti.** sah·deh·jeh gee·*deesh*/gee·*deesh* dur·*nyush* bee·leh·tee
How much?	**Ne kadar?** neh kah·dahr
Are there any discounts?	**İndirim var mı?** een·dee·reem vahr mih
Which...?	**Hangi...?** hahn·gee...
– gate?	**– kapı?** kah·pih
– lane?	**– hat?** haht
– platform?	**– peron?** peh·rohn
Where can I get a taxi?	**Nerede taksi bulabilirim?** neh·reh·deh tahk·see boo·lah·bee·lee·reem
Please take me to this address.	**Lütfen beni bu adrese götürün.** lyut·fehn beh·nee boo ahd·reh·seh gur·tyu·ryun
Where can I rent a car?	**Nereden bir araba kiralayabilirim?** neh·reh·dehn beer ah·rah·bah kee·rah·lah·yah·bee·lee·reem
Can I have a map?	**Bir harita alabilir miyim?** beer hah·reeh·tah ah·lah·bee·leer·mee·yeem

Ticketing

When's...to Istanbul?	**İstanbul'a...ne zaman?** ees·tahn·boo·lah... neh zah·mahn
– the (first) bus	**– (ilk) otobüs** (eelk) oh·toh·byus
– the (next) flight	**– (bundan sonraki) uçak** (boon·dahn sohn·rah·kee) oo·chahk
– the (last) train	**– (son) tren** (sohn) trehn

18

Where can I buy tickets?	**Nereden bilet alabilirim?** neh·reh·dehn bee·<u>leht</u> ah·lah·bee·lee·reem
One ticket/Two tickets, please.	**Bir/İki bilet lütfen.** beer/ee·<u>kee</u> bee·<u>leht</u> lyut·fehn
For *today/ tomorrow*.	**Bugün./Yarın.** <u>boo</u>·gyun/<u>yah</u>·rihn

▶ For days, see page 172.

▶ For time, see page 171.

A *one-way [single]/ round-trip [return]* ticket.	**Sadece *gidiş/gidiş dönüş* bileti.** <u>sah</u>·deh·jeh gee·<u>deesh</u>/gee·<u>deesh</u> dur·<u>nyush</u> bee·leh·<u>tee</u>
A *first/economy* class ticket.	***Birinci sınıf/Ekonomi sınıfı* bileti.** bee·reen·<u>jee</u> sih·<u>nihf</u>/eh·koh·noh·<u>mee</u> sih·nlh·<u>fih</u> bee·leh·<u>tee</u>
How much?	**Ne kadar?** <u>neh</u> kah·dahr
Is there a discount for...?	**...için indirim var mı?** ...ee·<u>cheen</u> een·dee·<u>reem</u> vahr mih
– children	– **Çocuklar** choh·jook·<u>lahr</u>
– students	– **Öğrenciler** ur·rehn·jee·<u>lehr</u>
– senior citizens	– **Yaşlılar** yash·lih·<u>lahr</u>
I have an e-ticket.	**Bir e-biletim var.** beer <u>eh</u>·bee·leh·teem vahr
Can I buy a ticket on the *bus/train*?	***Otobüste/Trende* bir bilet alabilir miyim?** oh·toh·byu·<u>steh</u>/trehn·<u>deh</u> beer bee·leht ah·lah·bee·<u>leer</u>·mee·yeem
I'd like to...my reservation.	**Reservasyonumu...istiyorum.** reh·zehr·vahs·yoh·noo·<u>moo</u>...ees·<u>tee</u>·yoh·room
– cancel	– **iptal etmek** eep·<u>tahl</u> eht·<u>mehk</u>
– change	– **değiştirmek** deh·yeesh·teer·<u>mehk</u>
– confirm	– **teyit etmek** teh·<u>yeet</u> eht·<u>mehk</u>

Plane

Getting to the Airport

How much is a taxi to the airport?	**Havaalanına bir taksi ne kadar?** hah·<u>vah</u>·ah·lah·nih·<u>nah</u> beer tahk·<u>see</u> neh kah·dahr
To...Airport, please.	**...havaalanına lütfen.** ...hah·<u>vah</u>·ah·lah·nih·<u>nah</u> <u>lyut</u>·fehn
My airline is...	**Havayolum...** hah·<u>vah</u>·yoh·loom...
My flight leaves at...	**Uçağım saat...kalkacak.** oo·chah·<u>ihm</u> sah·aht...kahl·kah·<u>jahk</u>

▶ For time, see page 171.

I'm in a rush.	**Acelem var.** ah·jeh·<u>lehm</u> vahr
Can you take an alternate route?	**Alternatif bir yol kullanabilir misiniz?** ahl·tehr·nah·<u>teef</u> beer yohl kool·lah·nah·bee·<u>leer</u>·mee·see·neez
Can you drive *faster/slower*?	**Daha *hızlı/ yavaş* kullanabilir misiniz?** dah·<u>hah</u> *hihz·<u>lih</u>/yah·<u>vash</u>* kool·lah·nah·bee·<u>leer</u>·mee·see·neez

You May Hear...

Hangi havayoluyla uçuyorsunuz? <u>hahn</u>·gee hah·<u>vah</u> yoh·<u>looy</u>·lah oo·<u>choo</u>·yohr·soo·nooz — What airline are you flying?

İç/Dış hatlar mı? <u>eech</u>/<u>dihsh</u> haht·<u>lahr</u> mih — Domestic/ International?

Hangi terminal? <u>hahn</u>·gee tehr·mee·<u>nahl</u> — What terminal?

You May See...

VARIŞ	arrivals
GİDİŞ	departures

BAVUL TESLİM BANDI	baggage claim
İÇ HAT UÇUŞLARI	domestic flights
DIŞ HAT UÇUŞLARI	international flights
UÇUŞ KAYDI MASASI	check-in desk
E-BİLET KAYDI	e-ticket check-in
ÇIKIŞ KAPILARI	departure gates

Check-in and Boarding

Where is check-in?	**Kayıt masası nerede?** kah·*yiht* mah·sah·*sih* *neh*·reh·deh
My name is...	**İsmim...** ees·*meem*...
I'm going to...	**...gidiyorum.** ...gee·*dee*·yoh·room
How much luggage is allowed?	**Ne kadar bavula izin var?** *neh* kah·dahr bah·voo·*lah* ee·*zeen* vahr
Which gate does flight...leave from?	**...numaralı uçak hangi biniş kapısından hareket edecek?** ...noo·*mah*·rah·lih oo·*chahk* *hahn*·gee bee·*neesh* kah·pih·sihn·*dahn* hah·reh·*keht* eh·deh·*jehk*

▶ For numbers, see page 169.

I'd like *a window/ an aisle* seat.	***Pencere/ Koridor* kenarı istiyorum.** pehn·jeh·*reh*/koh·ree·*dor* keh·nah·*rih* ees·*tee*·yoh·room
When do we *leave/ arrive*?	**Ne zaman *ayrılıyoruz/ varıyoruz*?** *neh* zah·man ie·rih·*lih*·yoh·rooz/vah·*rih*·yoh·rooz
Is there any delay on flight...?	**...uçuşunda herhangi bir gecikme var mı?** ...oo·choo·shoon·*dah* hehr·*hahn*·gee beer geh·jeek·*meh* vahr mih
How late will it be?	**Ne kadar gecikecek?** *neh* kah·dahr geh·jee·keh·*jehk*

▶ For time, see page 171.

21

You May Hear...

Bir sonraki! beer sohn·rah·<u>kee</u>

Next!

Lütfen, _biletiniz/ pasaportunuz_. lyut·fehn bee·leh·tee·<u>neez</u>/pah·sah·pohr·too·<u>nooz</u>

Your _ticket/ passport_, please.

Kaç parça bavulunuz var? <u>kach</u> pahr·<u>chah</u> bah·voo·loo·<u>nooz</u> vahr

How much luggage do you have?

Bavul ağırlığınız fazla. bah·<u>vool</u> ah·ihr·lih·ih·<u>nihz</u> fahz·<u>lah</u>

You have excess luggage.

El çantası için o çok _ağır/ büyük_. ehl chahn·tah·<u>sih</u> ee·<u>cheen</u> oh chohk ah·<u>ihr</u>/ byu·<u>yuhk</u>

That's too _heavy/ large_ for a carry-on [to carry on board].

Bu çantaları kendiniz mi hazırladınız? <u>boo</u> chan·tah·lah·<u>rih</u> kehn·dee·<u>neez</u> mee hah·zihr·lah·dih·<u>nihz</u>

Did you pack these bags yourself?

Taşımanız için herhangi bir şey verildi mi? tah·shih·mah·<u>nihz</u> ee·<u>cheen</u> hehr·<u>hahn</u>·gee beer <u>shay</u> veh·reel·<u>dee</u> mee

Did anyone give you anything to carry?

Ceplerinizi boşaltın. jehp·leh·ree·nee·<u>zee</u> boh·<u>shahl</u>·tihn

Empty your pockets.

Ayakkabılarınızı çıkarın. ah·<u>yahk</u>·kah·bih·lah·rih·nih·<u>zih</u> chih·<u>kah</u>·rihn

Take off your shoes.

Şu anda kalkan uçak... shoo ahn·<u>dah</u> kahl·<u>kahn</u> oo·<u>chahk</u>...

Now boarding flight...

Luggage

Where _is/are_...?   **...nerede?** ...<u>neh</u>·reh·deh

- the luggage carts [trolleys]   **– El arabaları** ehl ah·rah·bah·lah·<u>rih</u>

- the luggage lockers   **– Bagaj dolapları** bah·<u>gahj</u> doh·lahp·lah·<u>rih</u>

– the baggage claim	– **Bavul teslim bandı** bah·<u>vool</u> tehs·<u>leem</u> bahn·dih
My luggage has been lost.	**Bavulumu kaybettim.** bah·voo·loo·<u>moo</u> <u>kie</u>·beht·teem
My luggage has been stolen.	**Bavulum çalındı.** bah·voo·<u>loom</u> chah·lihn·<u>dih</u>
My suitcase was damaged.	**Bavulum hasar görmüş.** bah·voo·<u>loom</u> hah·<u>sahr</u> gurr·<u>myush</u>

Finding Your Way

Where *is/are*...?	**...nerede?** ...<u>neh</u>·reh·deh
– the currency exchange office	– **Döviz bürosu** dur·<u>veez</u> byu·roh·<u>soo</u>
– the car rental	– **Araba kiralama** ah·rah·<u>bah</u> kee·rah·lah·<u>mah</u>
– the exit	– **Çıkış** chih·<u>kihsh</u>
– the taxis	– **Taksiler** tahk·see·<u>lehr</u>
Is there...into town?	**Kente...var mı?** kehn·<u>teh</u>...<u>vahr</u> mih
– a bus	– **otobüs** oh·toh·<u>byus</u>
– a train	– **tren** trehn
– a subway [underground]	– **metro** <u>meht</u>·roh

▶ For directions, see page 33.

Train

How do I get to the train station?	**Tren garına nasıl gidebilirim?** trehn gah·rih·<u>nah</u> <u>nah</u>·sihl gee·deh·bee·<u>lee</u>·reem
Is it far?	**Uzak mı?** oo·<u>zahk</u> mih

Where *is/are*...?	...**nerede?** ...<u>neh</u>·reh·deh
– the ticket office	– **Bilet gişesi** bee·<u>leht</u> gee·sheh·<u>see</u>
– the luggage lockers	– **Bagaj dolapları** bah·<u>gahj</u> doh·lahp·lah·<u>rih</u>
– the platforms	– **Peronlar** peh·rohn·<u>lahr</u>

▶ For directions, see page 33.

▶ For ticketing, see page 18.

You May See...

PERONLARA	to the platforms
DANIŞMA	information
YER AYIRTMA	reservations
VARIŞ	arrivals
ÇIKIŞ	departures

Questions

Could I have a schedule [timetable], please?
Lütfen, bir tren tarifesi alabilir miyim? lyut·fehn beer <u>trehn</u> tah·ree·feh·<u>see</u> ah·lah·bee·<u>leer</u> mee·yeem

How long is the trip?
Yolculuk ne kadar sürüyor? yohl·joo·<u>look</u> neh kah·dahr syu·<u>ryu</u>·yohr

Do I have to change trains?
Aktarma yapmak gerekiyor mu? ahk·tahr·<u>mah</u> yahp·<u>mahk</u> geh·reh·<u>kee</u>·yohr moo

i The **Türkiye Cumhuriyeti Devlet Demiryolları (TCDD)** (Turkish Republic State Railways) operates in most regions of the country. Trains with sleeping cars are a good option for a long, overnight trip. For international travel, there are a number of express trains with separate first- and second-class cars. The cost of tickets for each differs by about 30%. For reduced rates on international travel, purchase an InterRail pass or a Balkan Flexipass. For domestic travel, be sure to inquire about train stops. Express trains generally connect large cities, while commuter trains are slower and make various stops along the route. Reservations may be made in advance via the TCDD website.

Departures

Which platform does the train to...leave from?	**...giden tren hangi perondan kalkıyor?** ...gee·<u>dehn</u> trehn hahn·<u>gee</u> peh·rohn·<u>dahn</u> kahl·<u>kih</u>·yohr
Is this the platform to...?	**...treni bu perondan mı kalkıyor?** ...treh·<u>nee</u> <u>boo</u> peh·rohn·<u>dahn</u> mih kahl·<u>kih</u>·yohr
Where is platform...?	**...peronu nerede?** ...peh·roh·<u>noo</u> <u>neh</u>·reh·deh
Where do I change for...?	**...için nerede aktarma yapacağım?** ...ee·cheen <u>neh</u>·reh·deh ahk·tahr·<u>mah</u> yah·pah·jah·<u>yihm</u>

Boarding

Is this seat taken?	**Bu koltuk dolu mu?** boo kohl·<u>took</u> doh·<u>loo</u> moo
I think that's my seat.	**Bu koltuk benim.** boo kohl·<u>took</u> beh·<u>neem</u>

You May Hear...

Lütfen yerlerinizi alın! <u>lyut</u>·fehn yehr·leh·ree·nee·<u>zee</u> ah·<u>lihn</u>	All aboard!
Biletler lütfen. bee·leht·<u>lehr</u> <u>lyut</u>·fehn	Tickets, please.
...aktarma yapmanız gerek. ...ahk·tahr·<u>mah</u> yahp·mah·<u>nihz</u> geh·<u>rehk</u>	You have to change at...
Bir sonraki durak... beer sohn·rah·<u>kee</u> doo·<u>rahk</u>...	Next stop...

Bus

Where's the bus station?	**Otobüs garajı nerede?** oh·toh·<u>byus</u> gah·rah·<u>jih</u> <u>neh</u>·reh·deh

26

How far is it?	**Ne kadar uzakta?** <u>neh</u> kah·dahr oo·zahk·<u>tah</u>
How do I get to...?	**...nasıl gidebilirim?** ...<u>nah</u>·sihl gee·deh·bee·<u>lee</u>·reem
Does the bus stop at...?	**Otobüs...duruyor mu?** oh·toh·<u>byus</u>... doo·<u>roo</u>·yohr moo
Could you tell me when to get off?	**İneceğim yeri söyler misiniz?** ee·neh·jeh·<u>yeem</u> yeh·<u>ree</u> sur·<u>ylehr</u> mee·see·neez
Do I have to change buses?	**Aktarma yapmam gerekiyor mu?** ahk·tahr·<u>mah</u> yahp·<u>mahm</u> geh·reh·<u>kee</u>·yohr moo
Stop here, please!	**Burada durun lütfen!** boo·rah·<u>dah</u> doo·roon <u>lyut</u>·fehn

▶ For ticketing, see page 18.

Turkish city buses are very inexpensive. Destinations are usually posted on the bus itself, but double check with the driver before boarding. In Istanbul, green buses are reserved for commuters and require payment in special tokens. Orange buses are public and tickets can be purchased on board. In Istanbul, it is a good idea to purchase an **akbil** (smart ticket) which allows you to buy credit to pay for bus, sea and subway/tunnel travel. Paying with an **akbil** gets you a discount of between 10-25%.

You May See...

OTOBÜS DURAĞI	bus stop
GİRİŞ/ÇIKIŞ	enter/exit
BİLETİNİZİ MÜHÜRLETİN	stamp your ticket

Subway [Underground]

Where's the nearest subway [underground] station?	**En yakın metro istasyonu nerede?** ehn yah·<u>kihn</u> <u>meht</u>·roh ees·tah·syoh·<u>noo</u> neh·reh·deh
Can I have a map of the subway [underground]?	**Bir metro planı verir misiniz?** beer <u>meht</u>·roh plah·<u>nih</u> veh·<u>reer</u> mee·see·neez
Which line for...?	**...için hangi hattı kullanmam gerekiyor?** ...ee·<u>cheen</u> <u>hahn</u>·gee haht·<u>tih</u> kool·lahn·<u>mahm</u> geh·reh·<u>kee</u>·yohr
Where do I change for...?	**...gitmek için nerede tren değiştirmeliyim?** ...geet·<u>mehk</u> ee·cheen <u>neh</u>·reh·deh <u>trehn</u> deh·yeesh·teer·meh·<u>lee</u>·yeem
Is this the right train for...?	**Bu tren...gidiyor mu?** boo trehn...gee·<u>dee</u>·yohr moo
Where are we?	**Neredeyiz?** <u>neh</u>·reh·deh·yeez

▶ For ticketing, see page 18.

Subway transportation is an option in Ankara and Istanbul at the moment. **Tünel** (Tunnel), the second-oldest subway in the world, first used in 1875, is located in Istanbul and travels between the Karaköy and Beyoğlu stations. Paying by **akbil** (smart ticket) will get you a discount on both subway and tunnel travel in Istanbul.

Boat and Ferry

When is the ferry to...?	**...araba vapuru saat kaçta?** ...ah·rah·<u>bah</u> vah·poo·<u>roo</u> sah·<u>aht</u> kahch·<u>tah</u>
Where are the life jackets?	**Can yelekleri neredeler?** jahn yeh·lehk·leh·<u>ree</u> <u>neh</u>·reh·deh·ler?

▶ For ticketing, see page 18.

You May See...

CANKURTARAN SANDALI	life boats
CAN YELEĞİ	life jackets

Turkey is essentially surrounded by water. That, combined with Turkey's habitual road traffic, makes boat travel an important alternative. The country's most important port is in Istanbul. **İstanbul Deniz Otobüsleri (IDO)** (Istanbul Sea Bus Company) provides regular catamaran and ferry service around Istanbul. Catamarans are generally more comfortable and faster, though it is more expensive to take a catamaran than a ferry. Denizline operates between Istanbul and Izmir and a number of operators provide ferry and car ferry service between Çeşme and Brindisi and Ancona, Italy. There are also a number of connections between Turkey and the Aegean Islands in summertime. **Akbil** (smart ticket) can also be used for sea travel, giving you a discount of between 10-25% on your travel.

Bicycle and Motorcycle

I'd like to rent [hire]...	**Bir...kiralamak istiyorum.** beer... kee·rah·lah·<u>mahk</u> ees·<u>tee</u>·yoh·room
– a bicycle	– **bisiklet** bee·seek·<u>leht</u>
– a moped	– **mopet** moh·<u>peht</u>
– a motorcycle	– **motorsiklet** moh·tohr·seek·<u>leht</u>
How much per day/week?	*Günlüğü/ Haftalığı ne kadar?* gyun·lyu·<u>yu</u>/ hahf·tah·lih·<u>ih</u> neh kah·dahr
Can I have a helmet/lock?	*Kask/ Kilit alabilir miyim?* kahsk/kee·<u>leet</u> ah·lah·bee·<u>leer</u> mee·yeem

29

Taxi

Where can I get a taxi?	**Nerede taksi bulabilirim?** neh·reh·deh tahk·<u>see</u> boo·lah·bee·<u>lee</u>·reem
I'd like a taxi *now/ for tomorrow* at...	***Şimdi/Yarın* saat...için bir taksi istiyorum.** <u>sheem</u>·dee/yah·<u>rihn</u> sah·<u>aht</u>...ee·<u>cheen</u> beer tahk·<u>see</u> ees·<u>tee</u>·yoh·room
Pick me up at....	**Beni...al.** beh·<u>nee</u>...<u>teh</u> ahl
Please take me to...	**Beni...götürür müsünüz lütfen.** beh·<u>nee</u>... gur·tyu·<u>ryur</u> myu·syu·nyuz <u>lyut</u>·fehn
– this address	**– bu adrese** boo ahd·reh·<u>seh</u>
– the airport	**– havaalanına** hah·<u>vah</u>·ah·lah·nih·<u>nah</u>
– the train station	**– tren garına** trehn gah·rih·<u>nah</u>
I'm late.	**Geciktim.** geh·jeek·<u>teem</u>
Can you drive *faster/slower*?	**Daha *hızlı/yavaş* kullanabilir misiniz?** dah·hah *hihz·<u>lih</u>/yah·<u>vahsh</u>* kool·lah·nah·bee·<u>leer</u> mee·see·neez
Stop/Wait here.	**Burada *durun/bekleyin.*** boo·rah·dah *<u>doo</u>·roon/behk·<u>leh</u>·yeen*
How much will it cost?	**Ne kadar tutar?** neh kah·dahr too·<u>tahr</u>
You said...lira.	**Siz...lira dediniz.** seez...lee·<u>rah</u> deh·dee·<u>neez</u>
Keep the change.	**Üstü kalsın.** yus·<u>tyu</u> kahl·<u>sihn</u>
A receipt, please.	**Fatura lütfen.** fah·<u>too</u>·rah <u>lyut</u>·fehn

▶ For numbers, see page 169.

▶ For time, see page 171.

You May Hear...

Nereye? <u>neh</u>·reh·yeh	Where to?
Adres nedir? ahd·<u>rehs</u> <u>neh</u>·deer	What's the address?

30

i
Turkish taxis are generally yellow, marked with the word **taksi** (taxi) on top and have a letter "T" on their license plates. Make sure that the meter is set to the correct rate: **gündüz** (day), from 6 a.m. to midnight, and **gece** (night), from midnight to 6 a.m. If you want to tip the driver, you can round up the fare. **Dolmuş** (group taxis) are an alternative to regular taxis. They follow specific routes, much like a bus, but stop at requested stops. They are cheaper than individual taxis.

Car

Car Rental [Hire]

Where can I rent [hire] a car?	**Nereden bir araba kiralayabilirim?** <u>neh</u>·reh·dehn beer ah·rah·<u>bah</u> kee·rah·lah·<u>yah</u>·bee·<u>lee</u>·reem
I'd like to rent [hire]...	**Bir...kiralamak istiyorum.** beer... kee·rah·lah·<u>mahk</u> ees·<u>tee</u>·yoh·room
– a 2-/4-door car	– ***iki/dört* kapılı araba** ee·<u>kee</u>/*durrt* kah·pih·<u>lih</u> ah·rah·<u>bah</u>
– an automatic car	– **otomatik araba** oh·toh·mah·<u>teek</u> ah·rah·<u>bah</u>
– a car with air conditioning	– **klimalı araba** <u>klee</u>·mah·lih ah·rah·<u>bah</u>
– a car seat	– **araba koltuğu** ah·rah·<u>bah</u> kohl·too·<u>oo</u>
How much...?	**...ne kadar?** ...<u>neh</u> kah·dahr
– per *day/week*	– **Günlüğü/Haftalığı** gyun·lyu·<u>yu</u>/ hahf·tah·lih·<u>ih</u>
– per kilometer	– **Kilometre başına** kee·loh·<u>meht</u>·reh bah·shih·<u>nah</u>
– for unlimited mileage	– **Sınırsız yakıt kullanımı** sih·nihr·<u>sihz</u> yah·<u>kiht</u> kool·lah·nih·<u>mih</u>
– with insurance	– **Sigortalı** sih·<u>gohr</u>·tah·lih

31

Are there any special weekend rates?	**Hafta sonu için indirim var mı?** hahf·<u>tah</u> soh·<u>noo</u> ee·<u>cheen</u> een·dee·<u>reem</u> vahr mih

You May Hear...

Uluslararası sürücü belgeniz var mı? oo·loos·<u>lahr</u>·ah·rah·sih syu·ryu·<u>jyu</u> behl·geh·<u>neez</u> <u>vahr</u> mih	Do you have an international driver's license?
Lütfen pasaportunuz. pas·sah·pohr·too·<u>nooz</u> <u>lyut</u>·fehn	Your passport, please.
Sigorta istiyor musunuz? sih·<u>gohr</u>·tah ees·<u>tee</u>·yohr moo·soo·nooz	Do you want insurance?
...ön ödeme var. ...<u>urn</u> ur·deh·<u>meh</u> vahr	There is a deposit of...
Burasını imzalayınız. boo·rah·sih·<u>nih</u> eem·zah·<u>lah</u>·yih·nihz	Please sign here.

Gas [Petrol] Station

Where's the gas [petrol] station, please?	**Benzin istasyonu nerede lütfen?** behn·<u>zeen</u> ees·tah·syoh·<u>noo</u> <u>neh</u>·reh·deh <u>lyut</u>·fehn
Fill it up, please.	**Depoyu doldurun lütfen.** deh·poh·<u>yoo</u> dohl·<u>doo</u>·roon <u>lyut</u>·fehn
...liters, please.	**...litre lütfen.** ...<u>lee</u>·treh <u>lyut</u>·fehn
I'll pay *in cash/by credit card*.	***Nakit/ Kredi kartı* ile ödeyeceğim.** nah·<u>keet</u>/ kreh·<u>dee</u> kahr·<u>tih</u> ee·leh ur·deh·yeh·<u>jeh</u>·yeem

You May See...

NORMAL	regular
SÜPER	premium [super]
DİZEL	diesel

Asking Directions

Is this the right road to...?	**Bu,...giden yol mu?** boo...gee·<u>dehn</u> yohl moo
How far is it to...?	**...buradan ne kadar uzakta?** ...boo·rah·<u>dahn</u> neh kah·dahr oo·zahk·tah
Where's...?	**...nerede?** ...<u>neh</u>·reh·deh
– ...Street	– **...caddesi** ...<u>jahd</u>·deh·see
– this address	– **Bu adres** boo ahd·<u>rehs</u>
– the highway [motorway]	– **Otoyol** oh·toh·<u>yohl</u>
Can you show me on the map?	**Bana haritada gösterebilir misiniz?** bah·<u>nah</u> hah·ree·tah·<u>dah</u> gurs·teh·reh·bee·<u>leer</u> mee·see·neez
I'm lost.	**Kayboldum.** <u>kie</u>·bohl·doom

You May Hear...

doğru ilerde <u>doh</u>·roo ee·lehr·<u>deh</u>	straight ahead
solda sohl·<u>dah</u>	on the left
sağda sah·<u>dah</u>	on the right
köşede/köşeyi dönünce kur·sheh·<u>deh</u>/ kur·sheh·<u>yee</u> dur·<u>nyun</u>·jeh	*on/around* the corner
karşısında kahr·shih·sihn·<u>dah</u>	opposite

arkasında ahr·kah·sihn·<u>dah</u>	behind
yanında yah·nihn·<u>dah</u>	next to
...sonra ...<u>sohn</u>·rah	after...
kuzey/güney koo·<u>zay</u>/gyu·<u>nay</u>	north/south
doğu/batı doh·<u>oo</u>/bah·<u>tih</u>	east/west
trafik ışıklarında trah·<u>feek</u> ih·shihk·lah·rihn·<u>dah</u>	at the traffic light
kavşakta kahv·shahk·<u>tah</u>	at the intersection

You May See...

STOP	**DUR**	stop
	YOL VER	yield
	PARK EDİLMEZ	no parking
	GİRİŞ YASAK	no entry
	TEK YÖN	one way
	YAYA GEÇİDİ	pedestrian crossing

Parking

Can I park here?	**Buraya park edebilir miyim?** <u>boo</u>·rah·yah pahrk eh·deh·bee·<u>leer</u> mee·yeem
Where is the nearest *parking garage/ parking lot [car park]*?	**En yakın *park yeri/ oto park* nerede?** ehn yah·<u>kihn</u> *pahrk* yeh·ree/oh·toh *pahrk* <u>neh</u>·reh·deh
How much...?	**...ne kadar?** ...<u>neh</u> kah·dahr
– per hour	**– Saatlik** sah·aht·<u>lihk</u>
– per day	**– Günlük** gyun·<u>lyuk</u>
– overnight	**– Bir gecelik** beer geh·jeh·<u>leek</u>

Breakdown and Repairs

My car *broke down/ doesn't start*.	**Arabam *bozuldu/ çalışmıyor.*** ah·rah·<u>bahm</u> *boh·zool·<u>doo</u>/chah·<u>lihsh</u>·mih·yohr*
Can you fix it?	**Onarabilir misiniz?** oh·nah·rah·bee·<u>leer</u> mee·see·<u>neez</u>
When will it be ready?	**Ne zaman hazır olur?** <u>neh</u> zah·mahn hah·<u>zihr</u> oh·<u>loor</u>
How much will it cost?	**Ne kadar para tutar?** <u>neh</u> kah·dahr pah·<u>rah</u> too·<u>tahr</u>

Accidents

There has been an accident.	**Kaza oldu.** kah·<u>zah</u> ohl·<u>doo</u>
Call *an ambulance/ the police*.	***Ambülans/ Polis* çağırın.** ahm·byu·<u>lahns</u>/ poh·<u>lees</u> chah·<u>ih</u>·rihn

Accommodations

Essential

Can you recommend a hotel?	**Bir otel tavsiye edebilir misiniz?** beer oh·<u>tehl</u> tahv·see·<u>yeh</u> eh·deh·bee·<u>leer</u>·mee·see·neez
I have a reservation.	**Yer ayırtmıştım.** yehr ah·yihrt·<u>mihsh</u>·tihm
My name is...	**İsmim...** ees·<u>meem</u>...
Do you have a room...?	**...odanız var mı?** ...oh·dah·<u>nihz</u> vahr mih
– for one/two	**– Bir/ İki kişilik** beer/ee·<u>kee</u> kee·shee·<u>leek</u>
– with a bathroom	**– Banyolu** bahn·yoh·<u>loo</u>
– with air conditioning	**– Klimalı** <u>klee</u>·mah·lih
For tonight.	**Bu gecelik.** <u>boo</u> geh·jeh·leek
For two nights.	**İki geceliğine.** ee·<u>kee</u> geh·jeh·lee·yee·<u>neh</u>
For one week.	**Bir haftalığına.** <u>beer</u> hahf·tah·lih·ih·<u>nah</u>
How much?	**Ne kadar?** <u>neh</u> kah·dahr
Do you have anything cheaper?	**Daha ucuz yer var mı?** dah·<u>hah</u> oo·<u>jooz</u> yehr <u>vahr</u> mih
When's check-out?	**Saat kaçta otelden ayrılmamız gerekiyor?** sah·<u>aht</u> kahch·<u>tah</u> oh·tehl·<u>dehn</u> ie·rihl·mah·<u>mihz</u> geh·reh·<u>kee</u>·yohr
Can I leave this in the safe?	**Bunu kasaya koyabilir miyim?** boo·<u>noo</u> kah·sah·<u>yah</u> koh·yah·bee·<u>leer</u> mee·yeem
Can I leave my bags?	**Eşyalarımı bırakabilir miyim?** ehsh·yah·lah·rih·<u>mih</u> bih·rah·kah·bee·<u>leer</u> mee·yeem

36

Can I have *the bill/ a receipt*?	**Fiş/ Hesap** alabilir miyim? <u>feesh</u>/heh·<u>sahp</u> ah·lah·bee·<u>leer</u> mee·yeem
I'll pay *in cash/ by credit card*.	**Nakit/ Kredi kartı** ile ödeyeceğim. nah·<u>keet</u>/ kreh·<u>dee</u> kahr·<u>tih</u> ee·leh ur·deh·yeh·<u>jeh</u>·yeem

A range of hotel choices are available in Turkey. In terms of more traditional options, you may choose to stay in **gençlik yurdu** (youth hostels), **pansiyon** (guest houses) or **otel** (hotels). Turkey, however, also offers a number of more special places to stay such as Ottoman mansions, historic houses, Cappadocian cave dwellings, seaside resorts, etc. If you arrive without accomodations, contact the **Turizm Danışma Bürosu** (tourist information offices) and they can help you with reservations.

Finding Lodging

Can you recommend a hotel?	**Bir otel tavsiye edebilir misiniz?** beer oh·<u>tehl</u> tahv·see·<u>yeh</u> eh·deh·bee·<u>leer</u> mee·see·neez
What is it near?	**Yakınında ne var?** yah·kih·nihn·<u>dah</u> <u>neh</u> vahr
How do I get there?	**Oraya nasıl gidebilirim?** oh·rah·yah <u>nah</u>·sihl gee·deh·bee·<u>lee</u>·reem

Otel (hotels) in Turkey are labeled with a government-assigned star system (one to five), which generally refers to the number of amenities offered and not how spectacular the hotel may be. Most double rooms are equipped with two twin beds, so if you want a bed for two, be sure to ask. Also, if you want a hotel with air-conditioning, book one that is three-stars or higher. For a more intimate taste of Turkish life, **pansiyon** (guest houses) offer rented rooms and breakfast is usually included in the price. Note that **gençlik yurdu** (youth hostels) are generally only open to card holders.

At the Hotel

I have a reservation.	**Yer ayırtmıştım.** <u>yehr</u> ah·yihrt·<u>mihsh</u>·tihm
My name is...	**İsmim...** ees·<u>meem</u>...
Do you have a room...?	**...odanız var mı?** ...oh·dah·<u>nihz</u> <u>vahr</u> mih
– with a *restroom [toilet]/shower*	– **Banyolu/Duşlu** bahn·yoh·<u>loo</u>/doosh·<u>loo</u>
– with air conditioning	– **Klimalı** <u>klee</u>·mah·lih
– that's *smoking/ non-smoking*	– **Sigara *içilen/ içilmeyen*** see·<u>gah</u>·rah ee·chee·<u>lehn</u>/ee·<u>cheel</u>·meh·yehn
For tonight.	**Bu gecelik.** <u>boo</u> geh·jeh·<u>leek</u>

Do you have a room...?	**...odanız var mı?** ...oh·dah·nihz vahr mih	
For two nights.	**İki geceliğine.** ee·kee geh·jeh·lee·yee·neh	
For one week.	**Bir haftalığına.** beer hahf·tah·lih·gih·nah	

▶ For numbers, see page 169.

Does the hotel have...?	**Otelde bir...var mı?** oh·tehl·deh beer...vahr mih
– a computer	– **bilgisayar** beel·gee·sah·yahr
– an elevator [a lift]	– **asansör** ah·sahn·surr
– (wireless) internet service	– **(kablosuz) internet hizmeti** (kahb·loh·sooz) een·tehr·neht heez·meh·tee
– room service	– **oda servisi** oh·dah sehr·vee·see
– a gym	– **jimnastik** jeem·nahs·teek
I need...	**Bana bir...lâzım.** bah·nah...liah·zihm
– an extra bed	– **ek yatak** ehk yah·tahk
– a cot	– **bebek yatağı** beh·behk yah·tah·gih
– a crib [child's cot]	– **çocuk yatağı** choh·jook yah·tah·gih

You May Hear...

Lütfen *pasaportunuz/ kredi kartınız*. lyut·fehn *pas·sah·por·too·nooz/kreh·dee kahr·tih·nihz*	Your *passport/ credit card*, please.
Bu formu doldurun lütfen. boo fohr·moo dohl·doo·roon lyut·fehn	Please fill out this form.
Burasını imzalayın lütfen. boo·rah·sih·nih eem·zah·lah·yihn lyut·fehn	Please sign here.

Price

| How much per night/week? | **Geceliği/ Haftalığı ne kadar?** geh·jeh·lee·<u>yee</u>/ hahf·tah·lih·<u>ih</u> neh kah·dahr |
| Does the price include breakfast/ sales tax [VAT]? | **Fiyata kahvaltı/ KDV dahil mi?** fee·yah·<u>tah</u> kah·vahl·<u>tih</u>/ kah·deh·<u>veh</u> dah·<u>heel</u> mee |

Questions

Where's...?	**...nerede?** ...<u>neh</u>·reh·deh
– the bar	**– Bar** bahr
– the bathroom [toilet]	**– Tuvalet** too·vah·<u>leht</u>
– the elevator [lift]	**– Asansör** ah·sahn·<u>surr</u>
Can I have...?	**...alabilir miyim?** ...ah·lah·bee·<u>leer</u> mee·yeem
– a blanket	**– Battaniye** baht·tah·nee·<u>yeh</u>
– an iron	**– Ütü** yu·<u>tyu</u>
– a pillow	**– Yastık** yahs·<u>tihk</u>
– soap	**– Sabun** sah·<u>boon</u>
– toilet paper	**– Tuvalet kağıdı** too·vah·<u>leht</u> kah·ih·<u>dih</u>
– a towel	**– Havlu** hahv·<u>loo</u>
Do you have an adapter for this?	**Bunun için bir adaptörünüz var mı?** boo·<u>noon</u> ee·cheen ah·dahp·tur·ryu·<u>nyuz</u> <u>vahr</u> mih
How do I turn on the lights?	**Işıkları nasıl açabilirim?** ih·shihk·lah·<u>rih</u> <u>nah</u>·sihl ah·chah·bee·<u>lee</u>·reem

Could you wake me at...? | **Beni saat...oyandırabilir misiniz?**
beh·<u>nee</u> sah·<u>aht</u>...oh·yahn·dih·rah·bee·<u>leer</u> mee·see·neez

▶ For time, see page 171.

Could I have my things from the safe? | **Kasadan eşyalarımı alabilir miyim?**
kah·sah·<u>dahn</u> ehsh·<u>yah</u>·lah·rih·mih ah·lah·bee·<u>leer</u>·mee·yeem

Is there *mail/ a message* for me? | **Benim için *posta/ mesaj* var mı?** beh·<u>neem</u> ee·cheen *pohs·<u>tah</u>/meh·<u>sahj</u>* <u>vahr</u> mih

You May See...

İTİNİZ/ÇEKİNİZ	push/pull
TUVALET	restroom [toilet]
DUŞ	shower
ASANSÖR	elevator [lift]
MERDİVENLER	stairs
ÇAMAŞIRHANE	laundry
RAHATSIZ ETMEYİNİZ	do not disturb
YANGIN KAPISI	fire door
ACİL ÇIKIŞ	emergency exit
ARAMA-UYANDIRMA	wake-up call

Problems

There's a problem. | **Bir sorun var.** beer soh·<u>roon</u> vahr

I've lost my *key/ key card.* | ***Anahtarımı/ Anahtar kartımı* kaybettim.**
ah·nah·tah·rih·<u>mih</u>/ah·nah·<u>tahr</u> kahr·tih·<u>mih</u> kie·beht·teem

I've locked myself out of my room.	**Kapıda kaldım.** kah·pih·<u>dah</u> kahl·<u>dihm</u>
There's no *hot water/toilet paper*.	***Sıcak su/ Tuvalet kağıdı yok.*** sih·<u>jahk</u> soo/too·vah·<u>leht</u> kah·ih·<u>dih</u> yok
The room is dirty.	**Oda kirli.** oh·<u>dah</u> keer·<u>leeh</u>
There are bugs in our room.	**Odamızda böcek var.** oh·dah·mihz·<u>dah</u> bur·<u>jehk</u> vahr
...has broken down.	**...kırık.** ...kih·<u>rihk</u>
Can you fix...?	**...tamir edebilir misiniz?** ...tah·<u>meer</u> eh·deh·bee·<u>leer</u>·mee·see·neez
– the air conditioning	– **Klimayı** <u>klee</u>·mah·yih
– the fan	– **Vantilatörü** vahn·tee·lah·tur·<u>ryu</u>
– the heat [heating]	– **Isıtıcıyı** ih·sih·tih·jih·<u>yih</u>
– the light	– **Işığı** ih·shih·<u>ih</u>
– the TV	– **Televizyonu** teh·leh·vee·zyoh·<u>noo</u>
– the toilet	– **Tuvaleti** too·vah·leh·<u>tee</u>
I'd like to move to another room.	**Başka bir odaya taşınmak istiyorum.** bahsh·<u>kah</u> beer oh·dah·<u>yah</u> tah·shihn·<u>mahk</u> ees·<u>tee</u>·yoh·room

 Turkish electricity is generally 220 volts, though 110 volts may be found in the European part of Istanbul. British and American appliances will need an adapter.

Check-out

When's check-out?	**Saat kaçta otelden ayrılmamız gerekiyor?** sah·<u>aht</u> kahch·<u>tah</u> oh·tehl·dehn ie·rihl·mah·<u>mihz</u> geh·reh·<u>kee</u>·yohr
Could I leave my bags here until...?	**Çantalarımı buraya...bırakabilir miyim?** chan·tah·lah·rih·<u>mih</u> boo·rah·<u>yah</u>... bih·rah·kah·bee·<u>leer</u> mee·yeem
Can I have *an itemized bill/ a receipt*?	***Dökümlü hesap/ Fiş* alabilir miyim?** dur·kyum·<u>lyu</u> heh·sahp/<u>feesh</u> ah·lah·bee·<u>leer</u> mee·yeem
I think there's a mistake in this bill.	**Sanırım bu hesapta bir yanlışlık var.** sah·<u>nih</u>·rihm <u>boo</u> heh·sahp·<u>tah</u> beer yan·lihsh·<u>lihk</u> vahr
I'll pay *in cash/by credit card*.	***Nakit/ Kredi kartı* ile ödeyeceğim.** nah·<u>keet</u>/ kreh·<u>dee</u> kahr·<u>tih</u> ee·leh ur·deh·yeh·<u>jeh</u>·yeem

Tipping in hotels is not necessary, but you may offer a few YTL to porters or to attentive staff for their help.

Renting

I've reserved *an apartment/ a room*.	**Bir *apartman/ oda* tuttum.** beer ah·pahrt·<u>mahn</u>/ oh·<u>dah</u> toot·<u>toom</u>
My name is...	**İsmim...** ees·<u>meem</u>...
Can I have the *key/ key card*?	***Anahtarı/ Anahtar kartını* alabilir miyim?** ah·nah·tah·<u>rih</u>/ah·nah·<u>tahr</u> kahr·tih·<u>nih</u> ah·lah·bee·<u>leer</u>·mee·yeem
Are there...?	**...var mı?** ...<u>vahr</u> mih
– dishes	**– Tabak çanak** tah·<u>bahk</u> chah·<u>nahk</u>

43

Are there...?	...var mı? ...vahr mih
– pillows	– **Yastık** yahs·<u>tihk</u>
– sheets	– **Çarşaf** chahr·<u>shahf</u>
– towels	– **Havlu** hahv·<u>loo</u>
When/Where do I put out the trash [rubbish]?	**Çöpü *ne zaman/ nereye* çıkarayım?** chur·<u>pyu</u> *neh* zah·mahn/neh·reh·<u>yeh</u> chih·kah·rah·yihm
...is broken.	...**bozuldu.** ...boh·zool·<u>doo</u>
How does...work?	...**nasıl çalışıyor?** ...<u>nah</u>·sihl chah·lih·<u>shih</u>·yohr
– the air conditioner	– **Klima** klee·<u>mah</u>
– the dishwasher	– **Bulaşık makinesi** boo·lah·<u>shihk</u> mah·kee·neh·<u>see</u>
– the freezer	– **Dondurucu** dohn·doo·roo·<u>joo</u>
– the heater	– **Isıtıcı** ih·sih·tih·<u>jih</u>
– the microwave	– **Mikrodalga** meek·roh·dahl·<u>gah</u>
– the refrigerator	– **Buzdolabı** <u>booz</u>·doh·lah·<u>bih</u>
– the stove	– **Fırın** fih·<u>rihn</u>
– the washing machine	– **Çamaşır makinesi** chah·mah·<u>shihr</u> mah·kee·neh·<u>see</u>

Household Items

I need...	...**ihtiyacım var.** ...eeh·tee·yah·<u>jihm</u> vahr
– an adapter	– **Adaptöre** ah·dahp·tur·<u>reh</u>
– aluminum [kitchen] foil	– **Alimünyum kağıdına** ah·lee·<u>myu</u>·nyoom kah·ih·<u>dih</u>·nah

– a bottle opener	– **Şişe açacağına** shee·<u>sheh</u> ah·chah·jah·ih·<u>nah</u>
– a broom	– **Süpürgeye** syu·pyur·geh·<u>yeh</u>
– a can opener	– **Konserve açacağına** kohn·<u>sehr</u>·veh ah·chah·jah·ih·<u>nah</u>
– cleaning supplies	– **Temizlik maddelerine** teh·meez·<u>leek</u> mahd·deh·leh·ree·<u>neh</u>
– a corkscrew	– **Şarap açacağına** shah·<u>rahp</u> ah·chah·jah·ih·<u>nah</u>
– detergent	– **Deterjana** deh·tehr·jah·<u>nah</u>
– dishwashing liquid	– **Bulaşık deterjanına** boo·lah·<u>shihk</u> deh·tehr·jah·nih·<u>nah</u>
– garbage [rubbish] bags	– **Çöp torbalarına** churp tohr·bah·lah·rih·<u>nah</u>
– a light bulb	– **Ampula** ahm·poo·<u>lah</u>
– matches	– **Kibrite** keeb·ree·<u>teh</u>
– a mop	– **Yer bezine** yehr beh·zee·<u>neh</u>
– napkins	– **Kağıt peçeteye** kah·<u>iht</u> peh·<u>cheh</u>·teh·yeh
– paper towels	– **Kağıt havluya** kah·<u>iht</u> hahv·loo·<u>yah</u>
– plastic wrap [cling film]	– **Plastik ambalaj kağıdına** plahs·<u>teek</u> ahm·bah·<u>lahj</u> kah·ih·dih·<u>nah</u>
– a plunger	– **Plançere** <u>plahn</u>·cheh·reh
– scissors	– **Makasa** mah·kah·<u>sah</u>
– a vacuum cleaner	– **Elektrikli süpürgeye** eh·lehk·treek·<u>lee</u> syu·pyur·geh·<u>yeh</u>

▶ For dishes and utensils, see page 68.

▶ For oven temperatures, see page 176.

Hostel

Do you have any places left for tonight?	**Bu gece için yer var mı?** boo geh·jeh ee·cheen yehr <u>vahr</u> mih
Can I have...?	**...alabilir miyim?** ...ah·lah·bee·<u>leer</u> mee·yeem
– a blanket	**– Battaniye** baht·tah·nee·<u>yeh</u>
– a pillow	**– Yastık** yahs·<u>tihk</u>
– sheets	**– Çarşaf** chahr·<u>shahf</u>
– towels	**– Havlu** hahv·<u>loo</u>
What time do you lock up?	**Kapılar saat kaçta kapanıyor?** kah·pih·<u>lahr</u> sah·<u>aht</u> kahch·<u>tah</u> kah·pah·nih·yohr

Hostels are located throughout Turkey and are a good option for those traveling through Turkey on a restricted budget. Keep in mind, though, that you usually need to be a card-holder in order to stay in a hostel.

Camping

Can I camp here?	**Burada kamp yapabilir miyim?** <u>boo</u>·rah·dah kahmp yah·pah·bee·<u>leer</u> mee·yeem
Is there a campsite near here?	**Yakınlarda bir kamp alanı var mı?** yah·<u>kihn</u>·lahr·<u>dah</u> beer <u>kahmp</u> ah·lah·nih <u>vahr</u> mih
What is the charge per *day/week*?	*Günlüğü/ Haftalığı* **ne kadar?** gyun·lyu·<u>yu</u>/ hahf·tah·lih·<u>ih</u> <u>neh</u> kah·dahr
Are there...?	**...var mı?** ...<u>vahr</u> mih
– cooking facilities	**– Pişirme olanakları** pee·sheer·<u>meh</u> oh·lah·nahk·lah·<u>rih</u>

– electrical outlets	**– Elektrik prizi** eh·lehk·<u>treek</u> pree·<u>zee</u>
– laundry facilities	**– Çamaşırhane** chah·mah·<u>shihr</u>·hah·<u>neh</u>
– showers	**– Duş** doosh
– tents for rent [hire]	**– Kiralık çadırlar** kee·rah·<u>lihk</u> chah·dihr·<u>lahr</u>
Where can I empty the chemical toilet?	**Portatif tuvaleti nereye dökebilirim?** pohr·tah·<u>teef</u> too·vah·leh·<u>tee</u> <u>neh</u>·reh·yeh dur·keh·bee·<u>lee</u>·reem

YOU MAY SEE...

İÇME SUYU	drinking water
KAMP YAPMAK YASAKTIR	no camping
ATEŞ/MANGAL **YAKMAK YASAKTIR**	no *fires/barbecues*

▶ For household items, see page 44.

▶ For dishes and utensils, see page 68.

Internet and Communications

Essential

Where's an internet cafe?	**İnternet kafe nerede?** een·tehr·<u>neht</u> kah·<u>feh</u> <u>neh</u>·reh·deh
Can I *access the internet/check e-mail* here?	**Burada *internete girebilir/ postalarımı kontrol edebilir* miyim?** <u>boo</u>·rah·dah een·tehr·neh·<u>teh</u> gee·reh·bee·<u>leer</u>/ pohs·tah·lah·rih·<u>mih</u> kohn·<u>trohl</u> eh·deh·bee·<u>leer</u> mee·yeem

How much per hour/half hour?	***Saati/Yarım saati ne kadar?*** *sah·ah·tee/ yah·rihm sah·ah·tee neh kah·dahr*
How do I connect/ log on?	***Nasıl bağlanabilirim/ girebilirim?*** nah·sihl *bah·lah·nah·bee·lee·reem/ gee·reh·bee·lee·reem*
I'd like a phone card, please.	**Bir telefon kartı lütfen.** beer teh·leh·fohn kahr·tih lyut·fehn
Can I have your phone number?	**Telefon numaranızı öğrenebilir miyim?** teh·leh·fohn noo·mah·rah·nih·zih ur·reh·neh·bee·leer mee·yeem

Here's my number/e-mail address.	**İşte *numaram/ e-posta adresim.*** eesh·teh noo·*mah*·rahm/eh·pohs·*tah* ahd·reh·seem
Call me.	**Beni arayın.** beh·*nee* ah·*rah*·yihn
E-mail me.	**Bana yazın.** bah·*nah* yah·zihn
Hello, this is...	**Merhaba, ben...** *mehr*·hah·bah behn...
I'd like to speak to...	**...ile konuşmak istiyorum.** ...ee·leh koh·noosh·*mahk* ees·*tee*·yoh·room
Can you repeat that, please?	**Tekrar eder misiniz lütfen?** tehk·*rahr* eh·*dehr* mee·see·neez *lyut*·fehn
I'll call back later.	**Daha sonra arayacağım.** dah·*hah* sohn·rah ah·rah·yah·*jah*·ihm
Goodbye. (said by first person)	**Hoşçakalın.** hosh·*chah* kah·lihn
Goodbye. (said by the other person)	**Güle güle.** gyu·*leh* gyu·*leh*
Where is the post office?	**Postane nerede?** pohs·tah·*neh* neh·reh·deh
I'd like to send this to...	**Bunu...göndermek istiyorum.** boo·*noo*... gurn·dehr·*mehk* ees·*tee*·yoh·room

Computer, Internet and E-mail

| Where's an internet cafe? | **İnternet kafe nerede?** een·tehr·*neht* kah·*feh* neh·reh·deh |
| Does it have wireless internet? | **Kablosuz internet var mı?** kahb·loh·*sooz* een·tehr·*neht* vahr mih |

How do I turn the computer *on/off*?	**Bilgisayarı nasıl *açabilirim/kapatabilirim*?** beel·gee·sah·yah·rih nah·sihl ah·chah·bee·lee·reem/ kah·pah·tah·bee·lee·reem
Can I...?	**...bilir miyim?** ...bee·leer mee·yeem
– access the internet here	**– Buradan internete bağlana** <u>boo</u>·rah·dahn een·tehr·neh·<u>teh</u> bah·lah·nah
– check e-mail	**– E-postaya baka** eh·poh·stah·yah <u>yah</u> bah·<u>kah</u>
– print	**– Basa** bah·<u>sah</u>
How much per *hour/half hour*?	**Saati/Yarım saati ne kadar?** sah·ah·<u>tee</u>/ yah·<u>rihm</u> sah·ah·<u>tee</u> <u>neh</u> kah·dahr
How do I...?	**Nasıl...?** <u>nah</u>·sihl...
– connect/ disconnect	**– bağlanırım/bağlantıyı keserim** bagh·lah·<u>nih</u>·rihm/bah·lahn·tih·<u>yih</u> keh·<u>seh</u>·reem
– log *on/off*	**– *giriş/çıkış* yaparım** gee·<u>reesh</u>/chih·<u>kihsh</u> yah·<u>pah</u>·rihm
– type this symbol	**– bu sembolü yazarım** <u>boo</u> sehm·boh·<u>lyu</u> yah·<u>zah</u>·rehm
What's your e-mail?	**E-posta adresiniz nedir?** eh·pohs·<u>tah</u> ahd·reh·see·<u>neez</u> <u>neh</u>·deer
My e-mail is...	**E-posta adresim...** eh·pohs·<u>tah</u> ahd·reh·<u>seem</u>...

You May See...

KAPAT	close
SİL	delete
E-POSTA	e-mail

ÇIKIŞ	logout
YARDIM	help
ANINDA MUHABBET	instant messenger
İNTERNET	internet
GİRİŞ	login
YENI MESAJ	new message

AÇ/KAPA	on/off
AÇİK	open
YAZDIR	print
KAYDET	save
GÖNDER	send
KULLANICI İSMİ/ŞİFRE	username/ password
KABLOSUZ İNTERNET	wireless internet

Phone

A *phone card/*
prepaid phone,
please.

Bir *telefon kartı/ kontörlü telefon* lütfen.
beer teh·leh·<u>fohn</u> kahr·<u>tih</u>/ kohn·tyur·<u>lyu</u>
teh·leh·<u>fohn</u> lyut·fehn

How much?

Ne kadar? <u>neh</u> kah·dahr

My phone doesn't
work here.

Telefonum burda çalışmıyor.
teh·leh·foh·<u>noom</u> boor·<u>dah</u>
chah·<u>lihsh</u>·mih·yohr

What's the
area/country code
for...?

...için *bölge/ ülke* kodu nedir? ...ee·<u>cheen</u>
burl·<u>geh</u>/ yul·<u>keh</u> koh·<u>doo</u> neh·deer

What's the number
for Information?

Bilinmeyen numaralar kaç?
bee·<u>leen</u>·meh·yehn noo·<u>mah</u>·rah·lahr <u>kahch</u>

I'd like the number
for...

...için numarayı istiyorum. ...ee·<u>cheen</u>
noo·<u>mah</u>·rah·yih ees·<u>tee</u>·yoh·room

Can I have your
number?

Telefon numaranızı öğrenebilir miyim?
teh·leh·<u>fohn</u> noo·<u>mah</u>·rah·nih·zih
ur·reh·neh·bee·<u>leer</u> mee·yeem

Here's my number.	**İşte numaram.**	eesh·<u>teh</u> noo·<u>mah</u>·rahm

▶ For numbers, see page 169.

Please call me.	**Lütfen beni arayın.**	<u>lyut</u>·fehn beh·<u>nee</u> ah·<u>rah</u>·yihn
Please text me.	**Lütfen bana yazın.**	<u>lyut</u>·fehn bah·<u>nah</u> <u>yah</u>·zihn
I'll call you.	**Sizi arayacağım.**	see·<u>zee</u> ah·rah·yah·<u>jah</u>·yihm
I'll text you.	**Size yazarım.**	see·<u>zeh</u> yah·<u>zah</u>·rihm

On the Phone

Hello, this is...	**Merhaba, ben...**	<u>mehr</u>·hah·bah <u>behn</u>...
I'd like to speak to...	**...ile konuşmak istiyorum.**	...ee·leh koh·noosh·<u>mahk</u> ees·<u>tee</u>·yoh·room
Extension...	**Dahili hattı...**	dah·<u>hee</u>·lee haht·<u>tih</u>...
Can you speak *louder*/*more slowly*, please?	**Daha *yüksek*/*yavaş* sesle konuşur musunuz lütfen?**	dah·<u>hah</u> yuk·<u>sehk</u>/yah·<u>vahsh</u> sehs·leh koh·noo·<u>shoor</u> moo·soo·nooz <u>lyut</u>·fehn
Can you repeat that, please?	**Tekrar eder misiniz lütfen?**	tehk·<u>rahr</u> eh·<u>dehr</u> mee·see·neez <u>lyut</u>·fehn
I'll call back later.	**Daha sonra tekrar ararım.**	dah·<u>hah</u> <u>sohn</u>·rah tehk·<u>rahr</u> ah·<u>rah</u>·rihm
Goodbye. (said by first person)	**Hoşçakalın.**	hosh·<u>chah</u> kah·lihn
Goodbye. (said by second person)	**Güle güle.**	gyu·<u>leh</u> gyu·<u>leh</u>

▶ For business travel, see page 142.

You May Hear...

Kim arıyor? keem ah·<u>rih</u>·yohr — Who's calling?

Bir dakika lütfen. beer dah·kee·<u>kah</u> <u>lyut</u>·fehn — Hold on, please.

Telefona gelemez. teh·leh·foh·<u>nah</u> geh·<u>leh</u>·mehz — *He/She* can't come to the phone.

Mesaj bırakmak istiyor musunuz? meh·<u>sahj</u> bih·rahk·<u>mahk</u> ees·<u>tee</u>·yohr moo·soo·nooz — Would you like to leave a message?

***Daha sonra/ On dakika içinde* arayın.** dah·<u>hah</u> <u>sohn</u>·rah/ohn dah·kee·<u>kah</u> ee·cheen·<u>deh</u> ah·<u>rah</u>·yihn — Call back *later/ in 10 minutes.*

Sizi tekrar arayabilir mi? see·<u>zee</u> tehk·<u>rahr</u> ah·rah·yah·bee·<u>leer</u> mee — Can *he/she* call you back?

Telefon numaranızı öğrenebilir miyim? teh·leh·<u>fohn</u> noo·<u>mah</u>·rah·nih·zih ur·reh·neh·bee·<u>leer</u> mee·yeem — What's your number?

Fax

Can I *send/receive* a fax here?	**Buradan faks *gönderebilir/ alabilir* miyim?** boo·rah·<u>dahn</u> <u>fahks</u> *gurn·deh·reh·bee·<u>leer</u>/ ah·lah·bee·<u>leer</u>* mee·yeem
What's the fax number?	**Faks numarası kaç?** fahks noo·<u>mah</u>·rah·sih kahch
Please fax this to...	**Lütfen bunu...fakslayın.** <u>lyut</u>·fehn boo·<u>noo</u>... fahks·<u>lah</u>·yihn

Post Office

Where's the *post office/mailbox [postbox]*?	***Postahane/ Posta kutusu* nerede?** pohs·tah·<u>neh</u>/pohs·<u>tah</u> koo·too·<u>soo</u> <u>neh</u>·reh·deh

A stamp for this *postcard/letter*, please.	**Bu *kartpostal/ mektup* için pul lütfen.** boo kahrt·pohs·*tahl*/mehk·*toop* ee·cheen pool lyut·fehn
How much?	**Ne kadar?** neh kah·dahr
I want to send this package by *airmail/express*.	**Bu paketi *uçak/ özel ulak* ile göndermek istiyorum.** boo pah·keh·*tee* oo·*chahk*/ ur·*zehl* oo·*lahk* ee·leh gurn·dehr·*mehk* ees·*tee*·yoh·room
A receipt, please.	**Lütfen bir fiş verin.** lyut·fehn beer feesh veh·reen

You May Hear...

Lütfen gümrük beyanını doldurunuz. lyut·fehn gyum·ryuk beh·yah·nih·nih dohl·doo·roo·nooz	Please fill out the customs declaration form.
Değeri nedir? deh·yeh·ree neh·deer	What's the value?
İçinde ne var? ee·cheen·deh neh vahr	What's inside?

Post offices in Turkey display a yellow sign with the letters **PTT (Posta Telegraf Telefon)** (Post Telegraph Telephone) in blue. Aside from sending letters or packages, you can also change money, make phone calls or buy phone cards. Major post offices in more touristic areas may stay open until midnight, with a more restricted schedule on Sunday. Smaller post offices are generally only open until 5 p.m.

▼ Food

Essential

Can you recommend a good *restaurant/bar*?	**İyi bir *lokanta/bar* önerebilir misiniz?** ee·<u>yee</u> beer loh·<u>kahn</u>·tah/bahr ur·neh·reh·bee·<u>leer</u> mee·see·neez
Is there *a traditional Turkish/ an inexpensive* restaurant near here?	**Yakınlarda *geleneksel Türk yemekleri/ ucuz yemek* sunan bir lokanta var mı?** yah·kihn·lahr·<u>dah</u> geh·leh·<u>nehk</u>·sehl tyurk yeh·mehk·leh·<u>ree</u>/oo·<u>jooz</u> yeh·<u>mehk</u> soo·<u>nahn</u> beer loh·<u>kahn</u>·tah <u>vahr</u> mih
A table for..., please.	**...kişi için bir masa lütfen.** ...kee·<u>shee</u> ee·cheen beer mah·<u>sah</u> lyut·fehn
Could we sit...?	**...oturabilir miyiz?** ...oh·too·rah·bee·<u>leer</u> mee·yeez
– here/there	**– Burada/Orada** <u>boo</u>·rah·dah/<u>oh</u>·rah·dah
– outside	**– Dışarda** dih·shah·rih·<u>dah</u>
– in a non-smoking area	**– Sigara içilmeyen bir yerde** see·gah·<u>rah</u> ee·<u>cheel</u>·meh·yehn beer yehr·<u>deh</u>
I'm waiting for someone.	**Birini bekliyorum.** bee·ree·<u>nee</u> behk·<u>lee</u>·yoh·room
Where are the restrooms [toilets]?	**Tuvalet nerede?** too·vah·<u>leht</u> <u>neh</u>·reh·deh
A menu, please.	**Menü lütfen.** meh·<u>nyu</u> <u>lyut</u>·fehn
What do you recommend?	**Ne önerirsiniz?** <u>neh</u> ur·neh·<u>reer</u>·see·neez
I'd like...	**...istiyorum.** ...ees·<u>tee</u>·yoh·room
Some more..., please.	**Biraz daha...istiyorum lütfen.** <u>bee</u>·rahz dah·<u>hah</u>...ees·<u>tee</u>·yoh·room <u>lyut</u>·fehn

Enjoy your meal.	**Afiyet olsun.** ah·fee·<u>yeht</u> ohl·soon
The check [bill], please.	**Hesap lütfen.** heh·<u>sahp</u> <u>lyut</u>·fehn
Is service included?	**Servis dahil mi?** <u>sehr</u>·vees dah·<u>heel</u> mee
Can I pay by credit card?	**Kredi kartı ile ödeme yapabilir miyim?** kreh·<u>dee</u> kahr·<u>tih</u> ee·leh ur·deh·<u>meh</u> yah·pah·bee·<u>leer</u> mee·yeem
Can I have a receipt, please?	**Lütfen fiş alabilir miyim?** <u>lyut</u>·fehn <u>feesh</u> ah·lah·bee·<u>leer</u> mee·yeem
Thank you.	**Teşekkür ederim.** teh·shehk·<u>kyur</u> eh·<u>deh</u>·reem

Restaurant Types

Can you recommend...?	**...önerebilir misiniz?** ...ur·neh·reh·bee·<u>leer</u> mee·see·neez
- a restaurant	**– Lokanta** loh·<u>kahn</u>·tah
- a bar	**– Bar** bahr
- a cafe	**– Kafe** kah·<u>feh</u>
- a fast-food place	**– Hazır yemek lokantası** hah·<u>zihr</u> yeh·<u>mehk</u> loh·<u>kahn</u>·tah·sih

Reservations and Questions

I'd like to reserve a table...	**...bir masa ayırtmak istiyorum.** ...beer mah·<u>sah</u> ah·yihrt·<u>mahk</u> ees·<u>tee</u>·yoh·room
- for two	**– İki kişi için** ee·<u>kee</u> kee·<u>shee</u> ee·cheen
- for this evening	**– Bu gece** <u>boo</u> geh·jeh
- for tomorrow at...	**– Yarın saat...için** yah·<u>rihn</u> sah·<u>aht</u>...ee·cheen

▶ For time, see page 171.

A table for two, please.	**İki kişilik bir masa lütfen.** ee·kee kee·shee·leek beer mah·sah lyut·fehn
We have a reservation.	**Yer ayırtmıştık.** yehr ah·yihrt·mihsh·tihk
My name is...	**İsmim...** ees·meem...
Could we sit...?	**...oturabilir miyiz?** ...oh·too·rah·bee·leer mee·yeez
– here/there	**– Burada/Orada** boo·rah·dah/oh·rah·dah
– outside	**– Dışarda** dih·shahr·dah
– in a non-smoking area	**– Sigara içilmeyen bir yerde** see·gah·rah ee·cheel·meh·yehn beer yehr·deh
– by the window	**– Pencere kenarında** pehn·jeh·reh keh·nah·rihn·dah
Where are the restrooms [toilets]?	**Tuvalet nerede?** too·vah·leht neh·reh·deh

You May Hear...

Rezervasyonunuz var mı? reh·zehr·vah·syoh·noo·nooz vahr mih	Do you have a reservation?
Ne kadar? neh kah·dahr	How many?
Sigara içilen bölümde mi içilmeyen bölümde mi? see·gah·rah ee·chee·lehn bur·lyum·deh mee ee·cheel·meh·yehn bur·lyum·deh mee	Smoking or non-smoking?
Siparişinizi vermeye hazır mısınız? see·pah·ree·shee·nee·zee vehr·meh·yeh hah·zihr mih·sih·nihz	Are you ready to order?
Ne istersiniz? neh ees·tehr·see·neez	What would you like?
...öneririm. ...ur·neh·ree·reem	I recommend...
Afiyet olsun. ah·fee·yeht ohl·soon	Enjoy your meal.

Eating Out

59

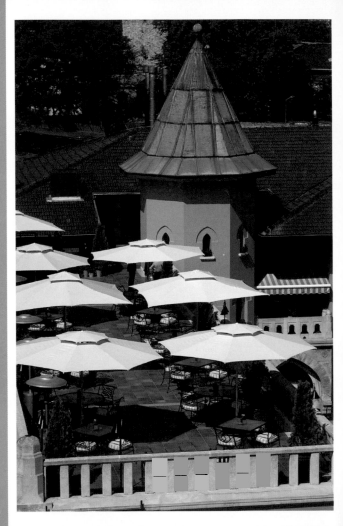

Ordering

Waiter!/Waitress!	**Garson!** gahr·<u>sohn</u>
We're ready to order.	**Siparişleri verebiliriz.** see·pah·reesh·leh·<u>ree</u> veh·reh·bee·<u>lee</u>·reez
May I see the wine list, please?	**Şarap listesini görebilir miyim lütfen?** shah·<u>rahp</u> lees·teh·see·nee gur·reh·bee·<u>leer</u> mee·yeem <u>lyut</u>·fehn
I'd like...	**...istiyorum.** ...ees·<u>tee</u>·yoh·room
– a bottle of...	**– Bir şişe...** beer shee·<u>sheh</u>...
– a carafe of...	**– Bir sürahi...** beer syu·<u>rah</u>·hee...
– a glass of...	**– Bir bardak...** beer bahr·<u>dahk</u>...

▶ For alcoholic and non-alcoholic drinks, see page 79.

The menu, please.	**Menü lütfen.** meh·<u>nyu</u> <u>lyut</u>·fehn
Do you have...?	**...var mı?** ...<u>vahr</u> mih
– a menu in English	**– İngilizce menü** een·gee·<u>leez</u>·jeh meh·<u>nyu</u>
– a fixed-price menu	**– Fiks menü** feeks meh·<u>nyu</u>
– a children's menu	**– Çocuk menüsü** choh·<u>jook</u> meh·nyu·<u>syu</u> <u>lyut</u>·fehn
What do you recommend?	**Ne önerirsiniz?** <u>neh</u> ur·neh·<u>reer</u>·see·neez
What's this?	**Bu nedir?** boo <u>neh</u>·deer
What's in it?	**İçinde ne var?** ee·cheen·deh <u>neh</u> vahr
Is it spicy?	**Baharatlı mı?** bah·hah·raht·<u>lih</u> mih
It's to go [take away].	**Paket olacak.** pah·<u>keht</u> oh·lah·<u>jahk</u>

You May See...

MASA ÜCRETİ	cover charge
FİKS MENÜ	fixed-price
MENÜ	menu
GÜNÜN MENÜSÜ	menu of the day
HİZMET DAHİL (DEĞİL)	service (not) included
SPESİYALLER	specials

Cooking Methods

baked	**fırında pişmiş** fih·rihn·<u>dah</u> peesh·meesh
boiled	**haşlanmış** hash·lahn·<u>mihsh</u>
braised	**hafif ateşte pişmiş** hah·<u>feef</u> ah·<u>tesh</u>·teh peesh·meesh
breaded	**ekmek kırıntıları ile kızartılmış** ehk·<u>mehk</u> kih·rihn·tih·lah·<u>rih</u> ee·leh kih·<u>zahr</u>·tihl·mihsh
creamed	**kremalı** kreh·mah·<u>lih</u>
diced	**kuşbaşı doğranmış** <u>koosh</u>·bah·shih doh·rahn·<u>mihsh</u>
filleted	**filetolanmış** fee·<u>leh</u>·toh·lahn·mihsh
fried	**kızartma** kih·zahrt·<u>mah</u>
grilled	**ızgara** ihz·gah·<u>rah</u>
poached	**haşlama** hahsh·lah·<u>mah</u>
roasted	**kızarmış** kih·zahr·<u>mihsh</u>
sautéed	**sote** soh·<u>teh</u>
smoked	**tütsülenmiş** tyut·syu·lehn·<u>meesh</u>
steamed	**buğulama** boo·<u>oo</u>·lah·<u>mah</u>
stewed	**yahni** yah·<u>hnee</u>

stuffed	**dolma** dohl·<u>mah</u>

Special Requirements

I'm...	**Ben...** behn...
– diabetic	– **şeker hastasıyım** sheh·<u>kehr</u> hahs·tah·<u>sih</u>·yihm
– lactose intolerant	– **laktoza duyarlıyım** lahk·toh·<u>zah</u> doo·yahr·<u>lih</u>·yihm
– vegetarian	– **vejetaryenim** veh·jeh·tahr·<u>yeh</u>·neem
I'm allergic to...	**...ya alerjim var.** ...yah ahl·lehr·<u>jeem</u> vahr

▶ For food items, see page 84.

I can't eat...	**...içeren yiyecek yiyemem.** ...ee·cheh·<u>rehn</u> yee·yeh·<u>jehk</u> yee·<u>yeh</u>·mehm
– dairy	– **Süt ürünleri** <u>syut</u> yu·ryun·leh·ree
– gluten	– **Glüten** glyu·<u>tehn</u>
– nuts	– **Kuruyemiş** koo·<u>roo</u>·yeh·meesh
– pork	– **Domuz eti** doh·<u>mooz</u> eh·<u>tee</u>
– shellfish	– **Kabuklu deniz ürünleri** kah·book·<u>loo</u> deh·<u>neez</u> yu·ryun·leh·<u>ree</u>
– spicy foods	– **Baharatlı yiyecekler** bah·hah·raht·<u>lih</u> yee·yeh·jehk·<u>lehr</u>
– wheat	– **Hamur işleri** hah·<u>moor</u> eesh·leh·<u>ree</u>
Is it *halal/kosher*?	*Helal/Kaşer* mi? heh·<u>lahl</u>/kah·<u>shehr</u> mee

Dining with Kids

Do you have children's portions?	**Çocuk porsiyonunuz var mı?** choh·<u>jook</u> pohr·see·yoh·noo·nooz <u>vahr</u> mih

A *highchair/child's* seat, please.	*Yüksek sandalye/ Çocuk sandalyesi* **lütfen.** yuk·<u>sehk</u> sahn·dahl·<u>yeh</u>/choh·<u>jook</u> sahn·dahl·yeh·<u>see</u> <u>lyut</u>·fehn
Where can I *feed/ change* the baby?	**Bebeği nerede** *besleyebilirim/ üstünü değiştirebilirim*? beh·beh·<u>yee</u> neh·reh·deh behs·leh·yeh·bee·<u>lee</u>·reem/yus·tyu·<u>nyu</u> deh·yeesh·tee·reh·bee·<u>lee</u>·reem
Can you warm this?	**Bunu ısıtabilir misiniz?** boo·<u>noo</u> ih·sih·tah·bee·<u>leer</u>·mee·see·neez

▶ For travel with children, see page 145.

Complaints

How much longer will our food be?	**Yemek için daha ne kadar bekleyeceğiz?** yeh·<u>mehk</u> ee·cheen dah·<u>hah</u> neh kah·dahr behk·leh·yeh·<u>jeh</u>·yeez
We can't wait any longer.	**Daha fazla bekleyemeyeceğiz.** dah·<u>hah</u> fahz·<u>lah</u> behk·leh·yeh·meh·yeh·jeh·yeez
We're leaving.	**Gidiyoruz.** gee·<u>dee</u>·yoh·rooz
I didn't order this.	**Benim siparişim bu değil.** beh·<u>neem</u> see·pah·ree·<u>sheem</u> boo deh·yeel
I ordered...	**...söyledim.** ...sur·yleh·<u>deem</u>
I can't eat this.	**Bunu yiyemem.** boo·<u>noo</u> yee·<u>yeh</u>·mehm
This is too...	**Bu çok...** boo <u>chohk</u>...
– cold/hot	– **soğuk/sıcak** soh·<u>ook</u>/sih·<u>jahk</u>
– salty/spicy	– **tuzlu/baharatlı** tooz·<u>loo</u>/bah·hah·raht·<u>lih</u>
– tough/bland	– **sert/yumuşak** sehrt/yoo·moo·<u>shahk</u>
This isn't *clean/ fresh*.	**Bu** *temiz/ taze* **değil.** boo teh·<u>meez</u>/tah·<u>zeh</u> deh·<u>yeel</u>

Paying

The check [bill], please.	**Hesap lütfen.** heh·sahp lyut·fehn
We'd like to pay separately.	**Ayrı ayrı ödemek istiyoruz.** ie·rih ie·rih ur·deh·mehk ees·tee·yoh·rooz
It's all together.	**Hepsi birlikte lütfen.** hehp·see beer·leek·teh lyut·fehn
Is service included?	**Servis dahil mi?** sehr·vees dah·heel mee
What's this amount for?	**Bu miktar ne için?** boo meek·tahr neh ee·cheen
I didn't have that. I had...	**Bunu almadım. ...aldım.** boo·noo ahl·mah·dihm...ahl·dihm
Can I pay by credit card?	**Kredi kartı ile ödeme yapabilir miyim?** kreh·dee kahr·tih ee·leh ur·deh·meh yah·pah·bee·leer mee·yeem
Can I have *an itemized bill/ a receipt*?	***Dökümlü hesap/ Fiş* alabilir miyim?** dur·kyum·lyu heh·sahp/feesh ah·lah·bee·leer mee·yeem
That was a very good meal.	**Yemek çok güzeldi.** yeh·mehk chohk gyu·zehl·dee

Tipping in restaurants is generally not necessary, but a tip of 5–10% in small establishments is appreciated. You may tip as much as 15% in a luxury restaurant. Be aware that the **kuver** (per-person cover charge) will already be added into the bill.

Market ———————————————————————

Where are the carts [trolleys]/ baskets?	***El arabaları/ Sepetler* nerede?** ehl ah·rah·bah·lah·<u>rih</u>/seh·peht·<u>lehr</u> neh·reh·deh
Where is...?	**...nerede?** ...<u>neh</u>·reh·deh

▶ For food items, see page 84.

I'd like some of that/those.	***Şundan/ Şunlardan* biraz istiyorum.** shoon·<u>dahn</u>/shoon·lahr·<u>dahn</u> beer·ahz ees·<u>tee</u>·yoh·room
Can I taste it?	**Tadına bakabilir miyim?** tah·dih·<u>nah</u> bah·kah·bee·<u>leer</u> mee·yeem
May I have...?	**...alabilir miyim?** ...ah·lah·bee·<u>leer</u> mee·yeem
– a *kilo/half-kilo* of...	**– ...dan *bir/yarım* kilo** ...dahn <u>beer</u>/yah·<u>rihm</u> kee·<u>loh</u>
– a *liter/half-liter* of...	**– ...dan *bir/yarım* litre** ...dahn <u>beer</u>/yah·<u>rihm</u> lee·<u>treh</u>
– a piece of...	**– ...bir parça** ...beer pahr·<u>chah</u>
– a slice of...	**– ...bir dilim** ...beer dee·<u>leem</u>
More/Less.	**Daha *fazla/ az.*** dah·<u>hah</u> fahz·<u>lah</u>/ahz
How much?	**Ne kadar?** <u>neh</u> kah·dahr
Where do I pay?	**Nereye ödeyeceğim?** <u>neh</u>·reh·yeh ur·deh·yeh·<u>jeh</u>·yeem
May I have a bag?	**Bir çanta, alabilir miyim?** beer chahn·<u>tah</u> ah·lah·bee·<u>leer</u> mee·yeem
I'm being helped.	**Yardım alıyorum.** yahr·<u>dihm</u> ah·<u>lih</u>·yoh·room

▶ For conversion tables, see page 175.

You May Hear...

Yardımcı olabilir miyim? yahr·dihm-<u>jih</u>
oh·lah·bee·<u>leer</u> mee·yeem

Can I help you?

Ne istersiniz? <u>neh</u> ees·<u>tehr</u>·see·neez

What would you like?

Başka bir şey? bahsh·<u>kah</u> beer shay

Anything else?

...lira. ...<u>lee</u>·rah

That's...lira.

In Turkey, there are a number of large supermarket and discount chains to shop in. They feature both local products as well as imported food. **Bakkal** (local grocery stores) can be found on just about every city block and offer enough to fill basic needs. There are also numerous specialty options: **çarşı** (small fruit and vegetable market), **balıkçı** (the fish store), and **kasap** (the butcher), in addition to the weekly **pazar** (neighborhood markets). In Istanbul be sure to visit the **Kapalı Çarşı** (covered bazaar) and the **Mısır Çarşısı** (spice bazaar).

You May See...

SON KULLANMA TARİHİ...	expiration date...
KALORİ	calories
YAĞSIZ	fat free
BUZDOLABINDA SAKLAYINIZ	keep refrigerated
...UFAK BİR MİKTARINI İÇEREBİLİR	may contain small traces of...
EN GEÇ...TARİHİNE KADAR SATILABİLİR	may be sold until...
VEJETARYENLER İÇİN UYGUNDUR	suitable for vegetarians

Dishes, Utensils and Kitchen Tools

bottle opener	**şişe açacağı** shee·<u>sheh</u> ah·chah·jah·<u>ih</u>
bowls	**çanak** chah·<u>nahk</u>
can opener	**konserve açacağı** kon·sehr·<u>veh</u> ah·chah·jah·<u>ih</u>
corkscrew	**şarap açacağı** shah·<u>rahp</u> ah·chah·jah·<u>ih</u>
cups	**fincan** fihn·<u>jahn</u>
forks	**çatal** chah·<u>tahl</u>
frying pan	**tava** tah·<u>vah</u>
glasses	**bardak** bahr·<u>dahk</u>
knives	**bıçak** bih·<u>chahk</u>
measuring *cup/ spoon*	**ölçü *kabı/ kaşığı*** url·<u>chyu</u> *kah·<u>bih</u>/ kah·shih·<u>ih</u>*
napkin	**kağıt peçete** kah·<u>iht</u> peh·<u>cheh</u>·teh
plates	**tabak** tah·<u>bakh</u>
pot	**çömlek** churm·<u>lehk</u>
saucepan	**tencere** tehn·<u>jeh</u>·reh
spatula	**spatula** spah·<u>too</u>·lah
spoons	**kaşık** kah·<u>shihk</u>

Meals

Breakfast

bal bahl	honey
ekmek ehk·<u>mehk</u>	bread

I'd like...	...**istiyorum.** ...ees·<u>tee</u>·yoh·room
More..., please.	**Daha...lütfen.** dah·<u>hah</u>...<u>lyut</u>·fehn

greyfurt gray·<u>foort</u>	grapefruit
küçük yuvarlak ekmek kyu·<u>chyuk</u> yoo·vahr·<u>lahk</u> ehk·<u>mehk</u>	rolls
kızarmış ekmek kih·zahr·<u>mihsh</u> ehk·<u>mehk</u>	roasted bread
marmelat mahr·meh·<u>laht</u>	marmalade
meyve suyu may·<u>veh</u> soo·yoo	fruit juice
portakal pohr·tah·<u>kahl</u>	orange
reçel reh·<u>chehl</u>	jam
süt syut	milk
tereyağı teh·<u>reh</u>·yah·ih	butter
...yumurta ...yoo·<u>moor</u>·tah	...eggs
– çırpma chihrp·<u>mah</u>	– scrambled
– katı kah·<u>tih</u>	– boiled
– sahanda sah·hahn·<u>dah</u>	– fried

Appetizers [Starters]

arnavut ciğeri ahr·nah·<u>voot</u> jee·yeh·<u>ree</u>	fried liver morsels
beyaz peynir beh·<u>yahz</u> pay·<u>neer</u>	white cheese
börek bur·<u>rehk</u>	hot filo pastries
dolma dohl·<u>mah</u>	stuffed grape leaves
imam bayıldı ee·<u>mahm</u> bah·yihl·<u>dih</u>	stuffed eggplant [aubergine]
patlıcan salatası paht·lih·<u>jahn</u> sah·<u>lah</u>·tah·sih	eggplant [aubergine] salad

With/Without...	...ile/-sız. ...<u>ee</u>·leh/·seez
I can't have...	...yiyemem. ...yee·<u>yeh</u>·mehm

69

pilaki pee·lah·<u>kee</u>   beans in olive oil

tarama tah·rah·<u>mah</u>   fish roe pâté

---

i **Meze** (appetizers) are the perfect accompaniment to
a leisurely drink before dinner. **Meze** may be hot, **sıcak
mezeler** (hot appetizers), or cold, **soğuk mezeler** (cold
appetizers). The selection that is served usually depends
on the main course to follow. Dried or marinated mackerel,
vegetables cooked in oil, tomato and cucumber salad or deep
fried mussels and calamari in sauce may precede grilled fish
or meat. Hummus, marinated stuffed eggplant, lentil balls or
spicy peppers with nuts might be served before a main dish of
kebab.

Soup

balık çorbası bah·<u>lihk</u> chohr·bah·sih   fish soup

et suyuna çorba eht soo·yoo·<u>nah</u> chohr·bah   consommé

kremalı çorba kreh·mah·<u>lih</u> chohr·<u>bah</u>   cream soup

patates çorbası pah·tah·<u>tehs</u> chohr·bah·<u>sih</u>   potato soup

sebze çorbası sehb·<u>zeh</u> chohr·bah·<u>sih</u>   vegetable soup

soğan çorbası soh·<u>ahn</u> chohr·bah·<u>sih</u>   onion soup

tavuk çorbası tah·<u>vook</u> chohr·bah·<u>sih</u>   chicken soup

Fish and Seafood

ahtapot ah·tah·<u>poht</u>   octopus

alabalık ah·<u>lah</u>·bah·<u>lihk</u>   trout

| I'd like... | **...istiyorum.** ...ees·<u>tee</u>·yoh·room |
| More..., please. | **Daha...lütfen.** dah·<u>hah</u>...<u>lyut</u>·fehn |

deniz tarağı deh·<u>neez</u> tah·rah·ih	clams
ıstakoz ihs·tah·<u>kohz</u>	lobster
istiridye ees·tee·<u>reed</u>·yeh	oysters
kalamar kah·lah·<u>mahr</u>	squid
karides kah·ree·<u>dehs</u>	shrimp [prawns]
lüfer lyu·<u>fehr</u>	bluefish
midye meed·<u>yeh</u>	mussels
morina balığı moh·<u>ree</u>·nah bah·lih·ih	cod
pisi balığı pee·<u>see</u> bah·lih·ih	plaice
ringa balığı reen·<u>gah</u> bah·lih·ih	herring [whitebait]
ton balığı <u>tohn</u> bah·lih·ih	tuna
kılıç şiş kih·<u>lihch</u> sheesh	swordfish kebabs grilled with bay leaves, tomatoes and green peppers
Çınarcık usulü balık chih·nahr·<u>jihk</u> oo·soo·<u>lyu</u> bah·<u>lihk</u>	fried swordfish, sea bass and shrimp, served with mushrooms
uskumru pilakisi oos·<u>koom</u>·roo pee·lah·kee·see	mackerel fried in olive oil, with potatoes, celery, carrots and garlic; served cold

WIth/WIthout...	...ile/-siz. ...<u>ee</u> leh/ sccz
I can't have...	...yiyemem. ...yee·<u>yeh</u>·mehm

71

Meat and Poultry

bonfile bohn·<u>fee</u>·leh	steak
böbrek bur·<u>brehk</u>	kidneys
but boot	leg
but eti boot eh·<u>tee</u>	rump
ciğer <u>jee</u>·ehr	liver
Çerkez tavuğu chehr·<u>kehz</u> tah·voo·oo	Circassian chicken: boiled chicken with rice and nut sauce
çiğ köfte chee kurf·<u>teh</u>	raw meatballs made from ground meat and cracked wheat
dana dah·<u>nah</u>	veal
domuz doh·<u>mooz</u>	pork
dana pirzolası dah·<u>nah</u> peer·zoh·lah·sih	T-bone steak
fileto fee·<u>leh</u>·toh	fillet
hindi heen·<u>dee</u>	turkey
jambon jahm·<u>bohn</u>	ham
kemikli et keh·meek·<u>lee</u> eht	cutlet
kuzu koo·<u>zoo</u>	lamb
kuzu dolması koo·<u>zoo</u> dohl·mah·<u>sih</u>	lamb stuffed with savory rice, liver and pistachios

I'd like...	**...istiyorum.** ...ees·<u>tee</u>·yoh·room
More..., please.	**Daha...lütfen.** dah·<u>hah</u>...<u>lyut</u>·fehn

kuzu güveç koo·<u>zoo</u> gyu·<u>vehch</u>

lamb stew with onions, garlic, potatoes, tomatoes and herbs

| With/Without... | ...ile/-siz. ...<u>ee</u>·leh/·seez |
| I can't have... | ...yiyemem. ...yee·<u>yeh</u>·mehm |

73

ördek ur·rdehk	duck
pirzola peer·zoh·lah	chops
sığır eti sih·ihr eh·tee	beef
sığır filetosu sih·ihr fee·leh·toh·soo	sirloin
sosis soh·sees	sausages
sülün syu·lyun	pheasant
şiş köfte sheesh kurf·teh	ground lamb croquettes on a skewer, grilled over charcoal
tavuk tah·vook	chicken
tavşan tahv·shahn	rabbit
yoğurtlu kebab yoh·oort·loo keh·bahb	kebab on toasted bread with pureed tomatoes and seasoned yogurt

i Turkish cuisine is complex, reflecting Turkey's situation as a crossroads where East meets West. You'll find there is a healthy emphasis on fresh meat, fish and vegetables mixed with spices. **Şiş kebab** (skewered cubes of meat) and **baklava** (filo pastry stuffed with honey and pistachio nuts) are two typical Turkish dishes known and enjoyed around the world today.

rare	**az pişmiş** ahz peesh·meesh
medium	**orta ateşte** ohr·tah ah·tehsh·teh
well-done	**iyi pişmiş** ee·yee peesh·meesh
I'd like...	**...istiyorum.** ...ees·tee·yoh·room
More..., please.	**Daha...lütfen.** dah·hah...lyut·fehn

Vegetable Dishes

imam bayıldı ee·<u>mahm</u> bah·yihl·<u>dih</u>

eggplant [aubergine] stuffed with tomatoes and cooked in olive oil; eaten cold

kabak musakkası kah·<u>bahk</u> moo·sahk·kah·sih

sautéed and fried eggplant [aubergine], green peppers, tomatoes, onions, zucchini [courgette] and ground meat

türlü tyur·<u>lyu</u>

cooked mixed vegetables and beans, served hot

i Dolma is the term for any stuffed vegetable. Stuffing may be made of a mix of ground meat, cheese, onion and tomato or may be a vegetarian rice stuffing with tomato, onion and garlic. Meat-filled dolma are usually served as a main course dish with yogurt sauce, while rice-filled dolma are usually cooked in olive oil and eaten at room temperature.

Vegetables

bezelye beh·<u>zehl</u>·yeh — peas

biber bee·<u>behr</u> — peppers

domates doh·mah·<u>tehs</u> — tomatoes

| With/Without... | ...ile/-siz. ...<u>ee</u>·leh/·seez |
| I can't have... | ...yiyemem. ...yee·<u>yeh</u>·mehm |

75

havuç hah·<u>vooch</u>	carrots
hıyar hih·<u>yahr</u>	cucumber
kabak kah·<u>bahk</u>	zucchini [courgette]
kereviz keh·reh·<u>veez</u>	celery
lahana lah·<u>hah</u>·nah	cabbage
mantar mahn·<u>tahr</u>	mushrooms
marul mah·<u>rool</u>	lettuce
patates pah·tah·<u>tehs</u>	potatoes
patlıcan paht·lih·<u>jahn</u>	eggplant [aubergine]
pirinç pee·<u>reench</u>	rice
sarı şalgam sah·<u>rih</u> shahl·gahm	rutabaga [swede]
sarmısak sahr·mih·<u>sahk</u>	garlic
soğan soh·<u>ahn</u>	onions
şalgam shahl·<u>gahm</u>	turnips
taze fasulye tah·<u>zeh</u> fah·<u>sool</u>·yeh	green beans
taze soğan tah·<u>zeh</u> soh·<u>ahn</u>	shallots [spring onions]

Spices and Staples

dere otu deh·<u>reh</u> oh·<u>too</u>	dill
karanfil kah·rahn·<u>feel</u>	cloves
kekik keh·<u>keek</u>	thyme

I'd like...	**...istiyorum.** ...ees·<u>tee</u>·yoh·room
More..., please.	**Daha...lütfen.** dah·<u>hah</u>...<u>lyut</u>·fehn

76

kırmızı biber kihr·mih·<u>zih</u> bee·<u>behr</u> chili

kimyon keem·<u>yohn</u> cumin

kişniş keesh·<u>neesh</u> cilantro

maydanoz mie·dah·<u>nohz</u> parsley

nane nah·<u>neh</u> mint

safran sahf·<u>rahn</u> saffron

Fruit

ahududu ah·hoo·doo·<u>doo</u> raspberries

çilek chee·<u>lehk</u> strawberries

elma ehl·<u>mah</u> apples

erik eh·<u>reek</u> plums

greyfurt gray·<u>foort</u> grapefruit

karpuz kahr·<u>pooz</u> watermelon

kavun kah·<u>voon</u> melon

kiraz kee·<u>rahz</u> cherries

muz mooz bananas

nar nahr pomegranates

portakal pohr·tah·<u>kahl</u> oranges

şeftali shehf·tah·<u>lee</u> peaches

üzüm yu·<u>zyum</u> grapes

| With/Without... | **...ile/-siz.** ...<u>ee</u>·leh/·seez |
| I can't have... | **...yiyemem.** ...yee·<u>yeh</u>·mehm |

Cheese

beyaz peynir beh·<u>yahz</u> pay·<u>neer</u>   white cheese

kaşar kah·<u>shahr</u>   hard cheese

otlu peynir oht·<u>loo</u> pay·<u>neer</u>   herb cheese

tulum peyniri too·<u>loom</u> pay·nee·<u>ree</u>   goat cheese

Dessert

aşure ah·<u>shoo</u>·reh   sweet, cold soup made of mixed grains, beans and dried fruits

ayva tatlısı ie·<u>vah</u> taht·lih·sih   baked quince slices in a syrup

baklava <u>bahk</u>·lah·vah   filo pastry filled with honey and pistachio nuts

kabak tatlısı kah·<u>bahk</u> taht·lih·sih   baked pumpkin in a syrup

kadayıf kah·<u>dah</u>·yihf   shredded wheat dessert, similar to baklava

kazandibi kah·<u>zahn</u>·dee·bee   oven-browned milk pudding

muhallebi moo·<u>hahl</u>·leh·bee   milk pudding

sütlaç syut·<u>lahch</u>   rice pudding

tavuk göğsü tah·<u>vook</u> gur·hsyu   milk pudding with thin filaments of chicken breast

The most common dessert after a meal is fresh seasonal fruit, though Turkish cooking offers a whole range of delights to try. Puddings, known as **muhallebi**, may or may not be milk-based and may be mixed with a variety of ingredients such as citrus fruit or even very thin slices of chicken breast. **Lokma** (dessert of fried dough dipped in syrup) and **helva** (sauteed flour and pine nuts mixed with milk and sugar or water) are also traditional desserts. The internationally-famous **baklava** (filo pastry stuffed with honey and pistachio nuts) is commonly eaten with coffee or after a kebab dish and the also well-known **lokum** (Turkish delight) is eaten as a digestive after meals.

Drinks

Essential

May I see the *wine list/ drink menu*, please?
Şarap listesini/ İçecek menüsünü görebilir miyim lütfen? *shah·rahp lees·teh·see·nee/ee·cheh·jehk meh·nyu·syu·nyu gur·reh·bee·leer mee·yeem lyut·fehn*

What do you recommend?
Ne önerirsiniz? *neh ur·neh·reer·see·neez*

I'd like a *bottle/ glass* of *red/white* wine.
Bir şişe/ bardak kırmızı/ beyaz şarap istiyorum. *beer shee·sheh/bahr·dahk kihr·mih·zih/beh·yahz shah·rahp ees·tee·yoh·room*

The house wine, please.
Ev şarabı lütfen. *ehv shah·rah·bih lyut·fehn*

Another *bottle/ glass*, please.
Bir şişe/ bardak daha lütfen. *beer shee·sheh/bahr·dahk dah·hah lyut·fehn*

May I have a local beer?	**Yerel bir bira alabilir miyim?** yeh·<u>rehl</u> beer bee·<u>rah</u> ah·lah·bee·<u>leer</u> mee·yeem
Let me buy you a drink.	**Size bir içki ısmarlayayım.** see·<u>zeh</u> beer eech·<u>kee</u> ihs·<u>mahr</u>·lah·yah·yihm
Cheers!	**Şerefe!** sheh·reh·<u>feh</u>
A *coffee/tea*, please.	***Kahve/ Çay* lütfen.** kah·<u>hveh</u>/ chie <u>lyut</u>·fehn
Black.	**Sütsüz.** syut·<u>syuz</u>
With milk.	**Sütlü.** syut·<u>lyu</u>
With sugar.	**Şekerli.** sheh·kehr·<u>lee</u>
With artificial sweetener.	**Yapay tatlandırıcılı.** yah·<u>pie</u> taht·<u>lahn</u>·dih·rih·jih·lih

..., please.	...lütfen. ...lyut·fehn
– Fruit juice	– **Meyve suyu** may·veh soo·yoo
– Soda	– **Soda** soh·dah
– (*Sparkling/Still*) Wine	– (*Maden/ Sade*) **Su** (mah·dehn/sah·deh) soo
Is the tap water safe to drink?	**Musluk suyu içilir mi?** moos·look soo·yoo ee·chee·leer mee

Non-alcoholic Drinks

ayran ie·rahn	natural yogurt drink
çay chie	tea
...kahve ...kah·hveh	coffee...
– **kafeini alınmış** kah·feh·ee·nee ah·lihn·mihsh	– decaffeinated
– **sütlü** syut·lyu	– with milk
– **sütsüz** syut·syuz	– black
kola koh·lah	soda
limonata lee·moh·nah·tah	lemonade
gazlı/gazsız **maden suyu** gahz·lih/gahz·sihz mah·dehn soo·yoo	*carbonated/non-carbonated* mineral water
salep sah·lehp	hot herbal drink
...suyu ...soo·yoo	...juice
– **ananas** ah·nah·nahs	– pineapple
– **domates** doh·mah·tehs	– tomato
– **portakal** pohr·tah·kahl	– orange
süt syut	milk

sütlü meyve suyu syut·<u>lyu</u> may·<u>veh</u> soo·yoo	milk shake
şalgam suyu shahl·<u>gahm</u> soo·yoo	turnip juice

---

i A number of non-alcoholic drinks are available in Turkey. Carbonated beverages and mineral water are easily found, though you may choose to enjoy a freshly-squeezed fruit juice, particularly in winter when citrus fruit is in season. And though Turkish coffee is internationally known, tea is more commonly drunk throughout the day. Black tea and herbal infusions are typical. Traditional drinks include **ayran** (yogurt drink), **boza** (fermented millet drink) and **sahlep** (wild orchid drink). **Ayran** is made by diluting yogurt and is often served with a pinch of salt added; it is a particularly refreshing drink in the summer. **Boza** and **sahlep** are only served in winter. **Boza** has a flavor similar to eggnog and **sahlep**, made from pulverized wild orchid roots, is sweet and is usually served with cinnamon sprinkled on top.

You May Hear...

Size bir içki alabilir miyim? see·<u>zeh</u> beer eech·<u>kee</u> ah·lah·bee·<u>leer</u> mee·yeem	Can I get you a drink?
Sütlü/Şekerli? syut·<u>lyu</u>/sheh·kehr·<u>lee</u>	With *milk*/*sugar*?
Gazlı/ *Gazsız* su? gahz·<u>lih</u>/gahz·<u>sihz</u> soo	*Carbonated*/*Non-carbonated* water?

Aperitifs, Cocktails and Liqueurs ————

cin jeen	gin
erikli konyak eh·reek·<u>lee</u> kohn·<u>yahk</u>	plum brandy, slivovitz
kayısılı konyak kah·yih·sih·<u>lih</u> kohn·<u>yahk</u>	apricot brandy

konyak kohn·<u>yahk</u>	brandy
viski vees·<u>kee</u>	whisky
votka voht·<u>kah</u>	vodka

Beer

bira bee·<u>rah</u>	beer
fıçı fih·<u>chih</u>	draft [draught]
şişe shee·<u>sheh</u>	bottled

Foreign spirits are available in Turkey, but the national drink is **raki** (aniseed liquor). Nearly 90-proof, it is usually drunk with a bit of added water. Adding water turns it a milky-white, which has earned the drink the nickname "lion's milk." Besides **raki**, Turkey also produces very good brands of dry red and white wine and a few types beer, of which Efes is the most common.

Wine

beyaz şarap beh·<u>yahz</u> shah·<u>rahp</u>	white wine
kırmızı şarap kihr·mih·<u>zih</u> shah·<u>rahp</u>	red wine
köpüklü şarap kur·pyuk·<u>lyu</u> shah·<u>rahp</u>	sparkling wine
pembe şarap pem·<u>beh</u> shah·<u>rahp</u>	blush [rosé] wine
sek şarap <u>sehk</u> shah·<u>rahp</u>	dry wine
tatlı şarap taht·<u>lih</u> shah·<u>rahp</u>	sweet wine

A number of grape varieties are grown in Turkey and the country has a long history of wine production. Each region specializes in a few particular types of wine, depending on the grapes that are grown there, so ask to try a local wine.

Menu Reader

i There are several different denominations of eating and drinking establishments in Turkey. **Restoran** (restaurant) used to be a term reserved only for the finest establishments, but now many different types of places use the name. **Lokanta** (family-run restaurants) are more economical and unpretentious. The food in **lokanta** is generally prepared in advance rather than to order and is often served cafeteria-style. **Meyhane** (taverns) are generally smoke-filled, noisy taverns that serve wine, **raki** (aniseed liquor) and **meze** (appetizers), while **birahane** (beer hall) are typical beer halls. **Kebapci** (kebab joint), **dönerci** (doner joint) and **pideci** (a place specializing in **pide**, Turkish-style pizza) are the Turkish equivalents of fast-food places.

Keep in mind that not all restaurants will present you with a menu upon sitting down, but may instead offer you something seasonal or the specialty of the house or may just begin bringing **meze** (appetizer). In many establishments a tray is brought and you can select what you would like. Know that you are not obligated to accept every plate the waiter brings. Though many people choose to make an entire meal out of **meze** (appetizers), if you'd like to try some of the delicious main dish options, don't forget to save some room! Remember that fish is also sold by weight, so feel free to request that the waiter weigh it beforehand.

ahtapot ah·tah·<u>poht</u>	octopus
ahududu ah·hoo·doo·<u>doo</u>	raspberry
alabalık ah·<u>lah</u>·bah·<u>lihk</u>	trout
ananas ah·nah·<u>nahs</u>	pineapple
arnavut ciğeri ahr·nah·<u>voot</u> jee·yeh·<u>ree</u>	fried liver morsels

aşure ah·<u>shoo</u>·reh

sweet, cold soup made of mixed grains, beans and dried fruits

ayran ie·<u>rahn</u>

natural yogurt drink

ayva tatlısı ie·<u>vah</u> taht·lih·sih

baked quince slices in a syrup

az pişmiş <u>ahz</u> peesh·meesh	rare
baklava <u>bahk</u>·lah·vah	filo pastry filled with honey and pistachio nuts
bal bahl	honey
balık çorbası bah·<u>lihk</u> chohr·bah·sih	fish soup
beyaz peynir beh·<u>yahz</u> pay·neer	white cheese
beyaz şarap beh·<u>yahz</u> shah·rahp	white wine
bezelye beh·<u>zehl</u>·yeh	peas
biber bee·<u>behr</u>	pepper
bira bee·<u>rah</u>	beer
bonfile bohn·fee·<u>leh</u>	steak
boza boh·<u>zah</u>	a calorie-packed, sour-tasting drink made from fermented millet
böbrek bur·<u>brehk</u>	kidney
börek bur·<u>rehk</u>	hot filo pastries
but boot	leg
but eti <u>boot</u> eh·tee	rump
ciğer <u>jee</u>·ehr	liver
cin jeen	gin
çay chie	tea

Çerkez tavuğu chehr·<u>kehz</u> tah·voo·oo — Circassian chicken: boiled chicken with rice and nut sauce

Çınarcık usulü balık chih·nahr·<u>jihk</u> oo·soo·<u>lyu</u> bah·<u>lihk</u> — fried swordfish, sea bass and shrimp, served with mushrooms

çırpma chihrp·<u>mah</u> — scrambled

çiğ köfte chee kurf·<u>teh</u> — raw meatballs made from ground meat and cracked wheat

çilek chee·<u>lehk</u> — strawberry

dana dah·<u>nah</u> — veal

dana pirzolası dah·<u>nah</u> peer·zoh·lah·sih — T-bone steak

deniz tarağı deh·<u>neez</u> tah·rah·ih — clams

dere otu deh·<u>reh</u> oh·<u>too</u> — dill

dolma dohl·<u>mah</u> — stuffed grape leaves

domates doh·mah·<u>tehs</u> — tomato

domuz doh·<u>mooz</u> — pork

ekmek ehk·<u>mehk</u> — bread

elma ehl·<u>mah</u> — apple

erik eh·<u>reek</u> — plum

erikli konyak eh·reek·<u>lee</u> kohn·<u>yahk</u> — plum brandy, slivovitz

et suyuna çorba eht soo·yoo·<u>nah</u> chohr·<u>bah</u>	consommé
ev şarabı <u>ehv</u> shah·rah·bih	house wine
fıçı fih·<u>chih</u>	draft [draught]
fileto fee·<u>leh</u>·toh	fillet
gazlı gahz·<u>lih</u>	carbonated water
gazlı maden suyu gahz·<u>lih</u> mah·<u>dehn</u> soo·yoo	carbonated mineral water
gazsız gahz·<u>sihz</u>	non-carbonated water
gazsız maden suyu gahz·<u>sihz</u> mah·<u>dehn</u> soo·yoo	non-carbonated mineral water
greyfurt gray·<u>foort</u>	grapefruit
havuç hah·<u>vooch</u>	carrot
hıyar hih·<u>yahr</u>	cucumber
hindi heen·<u>dee</u>	turkey
ıstakoz ihs·tah·<u>kohz</u>	lobster
içecek menüsünü ee·cheh·<u>jehk</u> meh·nyu·<u>syu</u>	drink menu
içki eech·<u>kee</u>	drink
imam bayıldı ee·<u>mahm</u> bah·yihl·<u>dih</u>	eggplant [aubergine] stuffed with tomatoes and cooked in olive oil
istiridye ees·tee·<u>reed</u>·yeh	oysters
iyi pişmiş ee·<u>yee</u> peesh·meesh	well-done
jambon jahm·<u>bohn</u>	ham

kabak kah·<u>bahk</u>
zucchini [courgette]

kabak musakkası kah·<u>bahk</u> moo·sahk·kah·sih
sautéed and fried eggplant [aubergine], green peppers, tomatoes, onions, zucchini [courgette] and ground meat

kabak tatlısı kah·<u>bahk</u> taht·lih·sih
baked pumpkin in a syrup

kadayıf kah·dah·<u>yihf</u>
shredded wheat dessert, similar to baklava

kafeini alınmış kah·feh·ee·<u>nee</u> ah·lihn·<u>mihsh</u>
decaffeinated

kahve kah·<u>hveh</u>
coffee

kalamar kah·lah·<u>mahr</u>
squid

karanfil kah·rahn·<u>feel</u>
cloves

karides kah·ree·<u>dehs</u>
shrimp [prawn]

karpuz kahr·<u>pooz</u>
watermelon

kaşar kah·<u>shahr</u>
hard cheese

katı kah·<u>tih</u>
boiled

kavun kah·<u>voon</u>
melon

kayısılı konyak kah·yih·sih·<u>lih</u> kohn·<u>yahk</u>
apricot brandy

kazandibi kah·<u>zahn</u>·dee·bee — oven-browned milk pudding

kekik keh·<u>keek</u> — thyme

kemikli et keh·meek·<u>lee</u> eht — cutlet

kereviz keh·reh·<u>veez</u> — celery

kılıç şiş kih·<u>lihch</u> sheesh — swordfish kebab grilled with bay leaves, tomatoes and green peppers

kırmızı biber kih·mih·<u>zih</u> bee·<u>behr</u> — chili

kırmızı şarap kihr·mih·<u>zih</u> shah·<u>rahp</u> — red wine

kızarmış ekmek kih·zahr·<u>mihsh</u> ehk·<u>mehk</u> — roasted bread

kimyon keem·<u>yohn</u> — cumin

kiraz kee·<u>rahz</u> — cherry

kişniş keesh·<u>neesh</u> — cilantro

kola <u>koh</u>·lah — soda

konyak kohn·<u>yahk</u> — brandy (cognac)

köpüklü şarap kyu·pyuk·<u>lyu</u> shah·<u>rahp</u> — sparkling wine

köpüksüz şarap kyu·pyuk·<u>syuz</u> shah·<u>rahp</u> — still wine

kremalı çorba kreh·mah·<u>lih</u> chohr·<u>bah</u> — cream soup

kuzu koo·<u>zoo</u> — lamb

kuzu dolması koo·<u>zoo</u> dohl·mah·<u>sih</u> — lamb stuffed with savory rice, liver and pistachios

kuzu güveç koo·<u>zoo</u> gyu·<u>vehch</u> — lamb stew with onions, garlic, potatoes, tomatoes and herbs

küçük yuvarlak ekmek kyu·<u>chyuk</u> yoo·vahr·<u>lahk</u> ehk·<u>mehk</u> — bread rolls

lahana lah·<u>hah</u>·nah — cabbage

leblebi lehb·leh·<u>bee</u> — roasted chick peas

limonata lee·moh·<u>nah</u>·tah — lemonade

lokum loh·<u>koom</u> — Turkish delight

lüfer lyu·<u>fehr</u> — bluefish

mantar mahn·<u>tahr</u> — mushroom

marmelat mahr·meh·<u>laht</u> — marmalade

marul mah·<u>rool</u> — lettuce

maydanoz mie·dah·<u>nohz</u> — parsley

meyve suyu may·<u>veh</u> soo·yoo — fruit juice

meze meh·<u>zeh</u> — appetizer

midye meed·<u>yeh</u> — mussels

morina balığı moh·<u>ree</u>·nah bah·lih·<u>ih</u> — cod

muhallebi moo·<u>hahl</u>·leh·bee — milk pudding

muz mooz — banana

nane nah·<u>neh</u> — mint

nar nahr — pomegranate

orta ateşte ohr·<u>tah</u> ah·tehsh·<u>teh</u> — medium

otlu peynir oht·<u>loo</u> pay·<u>neer</u> — herb cheese

ördek ur·rdehk	duck
patates pah·tah·tehs	potato
patates çorbası pah·tah·tehs chohr·bah·sih	potato soup
patlıcan paht·lih·jahn	eggplant [aubergine]
patlıcan salatası path·lih·jahn sah·lah·tah·sih	eggplant [aubergine] salad
pembe şarap pem·beh shah·rahp	blush [rosé] wine
pilaki pee·lah·kee	beans in olive oil
pirinç pee·reench	rice
pirzola peer·zoh·lah	chops
pisi balığı pee·see bah·lih·ih	plaice
portakal pohr·tah·kahl	orange
portakal suyu pohr·tah·kahl soo·yoo	orange juice
rakı rah·kih	spirit made from distilled grapes and aniseed, similar to French pastis or Lebanese arak
reçel reh·chehl	jam
ringa balığı reen·gah bah·lih·ih	herring [whitebait]
safran sahf·rahn	saffron
sahanda sah·hahn·dah	fried
salep sah·lehp	hot herbal drink
sarı şalgam sah·rih shahl·gahm	rutabaga [swede]

sarmısak sahr·mih·<u>sahk</u>		garlic
sebze çorbası sehb·<u>zeh</u> chohr·bah·<u>sih</u>		vegetable soup
sek şarap <u>sehk</u> shah·<u>rahp</u>		dry
sığır eti sih·<u>ihr</u> eh·tee		beef
sığır filetosu sih·<u>ihr</u> fee·<u>leh</u>·toh·soo		sirloin
soda soh·<u>dah</u>		soda
soğan soh·<u>ahn</u>		onion
soğan çorbası soh·<u>ahn</u> chohr·bah·sih		onion soup
sosis soh·<u>sees</u>		sausage
sülün syu·<u>lyun</u>		pheasant
süt syut		milk
sütlaç syut·<u>lahch</u>		rice pudding
sütlü syut·<u>lyu</u>		with milk
sütlü meyve suyu syut·<u>lyu</u> may·<u>veh</u> soo·yoo		milk shake
sütsüz syut·<u>syuz</u>		black
şalgam shahl·<u>gahm</u>		turnip
şalgam suyu shahl·<u>gahm</u> soo·yoo		turnip juice
şarap listesini shah·<u>rahp</u> <u>lees</u>·teh·see		wine list
şeftali shehf·tah·<u>lee</u>		peach
şeker sheh·<u>kehr</u>		sugar
şekerli sheh·kehr·<u>lee</u>		wIth sugar
şıra shih·<u>rah</u>		freshly pressed grape juice

şiş köfte <u>sheesh</u> kurf·<u>teh</u>	ground lamb croquettes on a skewer, grilled over charcoal
şişe shee·<u>sheh</u>	bottle
tarama tah·rah·<u>mah</u>	taramasalata, fish roe pâté
tatlı şarap taht·<u>lih</u> shah·<u>rahp</u>	sweet
tavşan tahv·<u>shahn</u>	rabbit
tavuk tah·<u>vook</u>	chicken
tavuk çorbası tah·<u>vook</u> chohr·bah·sih	chicken soup
tavuk göğsü tah·<u>vook</u> gur·hsyu	milk pudding with thin filaments of chicken breast
taze fasulye tah·<u>zeh</u> fah·<u>sool</u>·yeh	green beans
taze soğan tah·<u>zeh</u> soh·<u>ahn</u>	shallot [spring onion]
tereyağı teh·<u>reh</u>·yah·ih	butter
ton balığı <u>tohn</u> bah·lih·<u>ih</u>	tuna
tulum peyniri too·<u>loom</u> pay·nee·<u>ree</u>	goat cheese
türlü tyur·<u>lyu</u>	cooked mixed vegetables and beans, served hot
uskumru pilakisi oos·<u>koom</u>·roo pee·lah·kee·see	mackerel fried in olive oil, with potatoes, celery, carrots and garlic

üzüm yu·<u>zyum</u> — grapes

viski vees·<u>kee</u> — whisky

votka voht·<u>kah</u> — vodka

yapay tatlandırıcı yah·<u>pie</u>
taht·<u>lahn</u>·dih·rih·jih — artificial sweetener

yoğurtlu kebab yoh·oort·<u>loo</u> keh·<u>bahb</u> — kebab on toasted bread with pureed tomatoes and seasoned yogurt

yumurta yoo·<u>moor</u>·tah — egg

▼ People

Talking

Essential

Hello.	**Merhaba.** mehr·hah·bah
Hi!	**Selam!** seh·lahm
How are you?	**Nasılsınız?** nah·sihl·sih·nihz
Fine, thanks.	**İyiyim, teşekkürler.** ee·yee·yeem teh·shehk·kyur·lehr
Excuse me!	**Afedersiniz!** ahf·eh·dehr·see·neez
Do you speak English?	**İngilizce biliyor musunuz?** een·gee·leez·jeh bee·lee·yohr moo·soo·nooz
What's your name?	**İsminiz nedir?** ees·mee·neez neh·deer
My name is...	**İsmim...** ees·meem...
Pleased to meet you.	**Tanıştığımıza memnun oldum.** tah·nihsh·tih·ih·mih·zah mehm·noon ohl·doom
Where are you from?	**Nerelisiniz?** neh·reh·lee·see·neez
I'm from the U.S./U.K.	**Amerikadanım/Birleşik Krallıktanım.** ah·meh·ree·kah·dah·nihm/beer·leh·sheek krahl·lihk·tah·nihm
What do you do?	**Ne iş yapıyorsunuz?** neh eesh yah·pih·yohr·soo·nooz
I work for...	**...için çalışıyorum.** ...ee·cheen chah·lih·shih·yoh·room
I'm a student.	**Öğrenciyim.** ur·rehn·jee·eem
I'm retired.	**Emekliyim.** eh·mehk·lee·yeem
Do you like...?	**...sever misiniz?** ...seh·vehr mee·see·neez

Goodbye. (said by departing persons)	**Hoşçakalın.** hosh·_chah_ kah·lihn
Goodbye. (said by persons staying behind)	**Güle güle.** gyu·_leh_ gyu·_leh_
See you later.	**Tekrar görüşmek üzere.** tehk·_rahr_ gur·ryush·_mehk_ yu·zeh·reh

i When formally addressing someone, it is polite to use the person's first name followed by either **Hanım** (polite address for women) or **Bey** (polite address for men). So Ali and his wife Binnur would be addressed as Ali Bey and Binnur Hanım, respectively. **Bay** (polite address for male foreigners) and **Bayan** (polite address for female foreigners) are also used, particularly for non-Muslims. In business settings, **Sayin** (polite address for men and women in a business setting) is commonly used followed by the last name. For example, Ali Kandemir would be addressed as Sayin Kandemir.

Communication Difficulties

Do you speak English?	**İngilizce biliyor musunuz?** een·gee·_leez_·jeh bee·_lee_·yohr moo·soo·nooz
Does anyone here speak English?	**Burada İngilizce konuşan biri var mı?** _boo_·rah·dah een·gee·_leez_·jeh koh·_noo_·shahn bee·ree _vahr_ mih
I don't speak Turkish.	**Türkçe bilmiyorum.** _tyurk_·cheh _beel_·mee·yoh·room
Can you speak more slowly?	**Daha yavaş konuşur musunuz lütfen?** dah·_hah_ yah·vahsh koh·noo·shoor moo·soo·nooz _lyut_·fehn
Can you repeat that?	**Tekrar eder misiniz lütfen?** tekh·_rahr_ eh·_dehr_ mee·see·neez _lyut_·fehn

Excuse me?	**Efendim?** eh·*fehn*·deem
What was that?	**O neydi?** oh *nay*·dee
Write it down, please.	**Lütfen yazar mısınız.** *lyut*·fehn yah·*zahr* mih·sih·nihz
Can you translate this for me?	**Bunu benim için tercüme eder misiniz?** boo·*noo* beh·*neem* ee·cheen tehr·jyu·*meh* eh·*dehr* mee·see·neez
What does *this/ that* mean?	*Bu/O* **ne demek?** *boo/oh* *neh* deh·mehk
I understand.	**Anladım.** ahn·lah·*dihm*
I don't understand.	**Anlamadım.** ahn·*lah*·mah·dihm
Do you understand?	**Anladınız mı?** anh·lah·dih·*nihz* mih

You May Hear...

| **Sadece çok az İngilizce konuşuyorum.** *sah*·deh·jeh chohk *ahz* een·geh·*leez*·jeh koh·noo·*shoo*·yoh·room | I only speak a little English. |
| **İngilizce konuşmuyorum.** een·gee·*leez*·jeh koh·*noosh*·moo·yoh·room | I don't speak English. |

Making Friends

Hello.	**Merhaba.** *mehr*·hah·bah
Hi!	**Selam!** seh·*lahm*
Good morning.	**Günaydın.** gyu·nie·*dihn*
Good afternoon.	**İyi günler.** ee·*yee* gyun·*lehr*
Good evening.	**İyi akşamlar.** ee·*yee* ahk·*shahm*·lahr
My name is...	**İsmim...** ees·*meem*...

What's your name?	**İsminiz nedir?** ees·mee·neez neh·deer
I'd like to introduce you to...	**Sizi...ile tanıştırmak istiyorum.** see·zee... ee·leh tah·nihsh·tihr·mahk ees·tee·yoh·room
Nice to meet you.	**Tanıştığımıza memnun oldum.** tah·nihsh·tih·ih·mih·zah mehm·noon ohl·doom
How are you?	**Nasılsınız?** nah·sihl·sih·nihz
Fine, thanks.	**İyiyim, teşekkürler.** ee·yee·yeem teh·shehk·kyur·lehr
And you?	**Siz?** seez

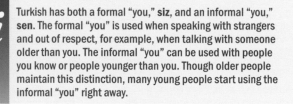

Turkish has both a formal "you," **siz**, and an informal "you," **sen**. The formal "you" is used when speaking with strangers and out of respect, for example, when talking with someone older than you. The informal "you" can be used with people you know or people younger than you. Though older people maintain this distinction, many young people start using the informal "you" right away.

Travel Talk

I'm here...	**...amacıyla buradayım.** ...ah·mah·jihy·lah boo·rah·dah·yihm
– on business	– **İş** eesh
– on vacation [holiday]	– **Tatil** tah·teel
– studying	– **Okumak** oh·koo·mahk
I'm staying for...	**...için kalıyorum.** ...ee·cheen kah·lih·yoh·room
I've been here...	**...burdayım.** ...boor·dah·yihm
– a day	– **Bir gündür** beer gyun·dyur

– a week	**– Bir haftadır** beer hahf·<u>tah</u>·dihr
– a month	**– Bir aydır** beer <u>ie</u>·dihr

▸ For numbers, see page 169.

Where are you from?	**Nerelisiniz?** <u>neh</u>·reh·lee·see·neez
I'm from...	**...-denim.** ...<u>deh</u>·neem

Relationships

Who are you with?	**Kiminlesiniz?** kee·<u>meen</u>·leh·see·neez
I'm on my own.	**Tek başımayım.** <u>tehk</u> bah·shih·<u>mah</u>·yihm
I'm with...	**...ile birlikteyim.** ...ee·<u>leh</u> beer·leek·<u>teh</u>·yeem
– my *husband/wife*	**– Kocam/Karım** koh·<u>jahm</u>/kah·<u>rihm</u>
– my *boyfriend/ girlfriend*	**– *Erkek/Kız* arkadaşım** ehr·<u>kehk</u>/<u>kihz</u> ahr·kah·dah·shihm

I'm with...	...ile birlikteyim. ...ee·<u>leh</u> beer·leek·<u>teh</u>·yeem
– a friend	– **Bir arkadaş** beer ahr·kah·<u>dahsh</u>
– a colleague	– **Bir meslektaş** beer mehs·lehk·<u>tahsh</u>
When's your birthday?	**Doğum gününüz ne zaman?** doh·<u>oom</u> gyu·nyu·<u>nyuz</u> neh zah·mahn
How old are you?	**Kaç yaşındasınız?** <u>kahch</u> yah·shihn·<u>dah</u>·sih·nihz
I'm...	...**yaşındayım.** ...yah·shihn·<u>dah</u>·yihm

▶ For numbers, see page 169.

Are you married?	**Evli misiniz?** ehv·<u>lee</u> mee·see·neez
I'm single.	**Bekârım.** beh·<u>kah</u>·rihm
I'm married.	**Evliyim.** ehv·<u>lee</u>·yeem
I'm divorced.	**Boşanmışım.** boh·shan·<u>mih</u>·shihm
I'm separated.	**Ayrıyım.** ie·<u>rih</u>·yihm
I'm in a relationship.	**Beraberliğim var.** beh·rah·behr·lee·<u>eem</u> vahr
I'm widowed.	**Dulum.** <u>doo</u>·loom
Do you have *children/ grandchildren*?	*Çocuğunuz/ Torununuz* var mı? choh·joo·**oo**·<u>nooz</u>/toh·roo·noo·<u>nooz</u> vahr mih

Work and School

What do you do?	**Ne iş yapıyorsunuz?** <u>neh</u> eesh yah·<u>pih</u>·yohr·soo·nooz
What are you studying?	**Ne okuyorsunuz?** <u>neh</u> oh·<u>koo</u>·yohr·soo·nooz
I'm studying...	...**okuyorum.** ...oh·<u>koo</u>·yoh·room

I work *full/part* time.	**Tam/Yarım zamanlı çalışıyorum.** *tahm/ yah·rihm* zah·mahn·lih chah·lih·<u>shih</u>·yoh·room
I'm between jobs.	**İşten yeni ayrıldım.** eesh·<u>tehn</u> yeh·<u>nee</u> ie·rihl·<u>deem</u>
I work at home.	**Evde çalışıyorum.** ehv·<u>deh</u> chah·lih·<u>shih</u>·yoh·room
Who do you work for?	**Kimin için çalışıyorsunuz?** kee·<u>meen</u> ee·cheen chah·lih·<u>shih</u>·yohr·soo·nooz
I work for...	**...için çalışıyorum.** ...ee·<u>cheen</u> chah·lih·<u>shih</u>·yoh·room
Here's my business card.	**Buyrun, kartvizitim.** <u>booy</u>·roon <u>cahrt</u>·vee·zee·<u>teem</u>

▶ For business travel, see page 142.

Weather

What is the weather forecast for tomorrow?	**Yarın için hava tahmini nasıl?** <u>yah</u>·rihn ee·cheen hah·<u>vah</u> tah·mee·<u>nee</u> nah·sihl
What *beautiful/ terrible* weather!	**Ne kadar *güzel/kötü* bir hava!** <u>neh</u> kah·dahr gyu·<u>zehl</u>/kur·<u>tyu</u> beer hah·<u>vah</u>
It's *cool/warm*.	**Serin./Ilık.** seh·<u>reen</u>/ih·<u>lihk</u>
It's *rainy/sunny*.	**Yağmurlu./Güneşli.** yah·moor·<u>loo</u>/ gyu·nehsh·<u>lee</u>
It's *snowy/icy*.	**Karlı./Buzlu.** kahr·<u>lih</u>/booz·<u>loo</u>
Do I need *a jacket/ an umbrella*?	***Monta/Şemsiyeye* ihtiyacım var mı?** *mohn·<u>tah</u>/shehm·see·yeh·<u>yeh</u>* eeh·tee·yah·<u>jihm</u> vahr mih

▶ For temperature, see page 176.

103

Romance

Essential

Would you like to go out for a *drink/meal*?	**Dışarı çıkıp birşeyler *içmek/yemek* ister misiniz?** dih·shah·_rih_ chih·kihp beer shay·lehr eech·_mehk_/yeh·_mehk_ ees·tehr mee·see·neez
What are your plans for *tonight/tomorrow*?	**Bu *gece/yarın* için planınız ne?** boo geh·_jeh_/yah·_rinn_ ee·cheen plah·nih·_nihz_ neh
Can I have your number?	**Telefon numaranızı öğrenebilir miyim?** teh·leh·_fohn_ noo·_mah_·rah·nih·_zih_ ur·reh·neh·bee·leer mee·yeem
Can I join you?	**Size katılabilir miyim?** see·_zeh_ kah·tih·lah·bee·leer mee·yeem
Let me buy you a drink.	**Size bir içki ısmarlayayım.** see·_zeh_ beer eech·_kee_ ihs·mahr·lah·yah·_yihm_
I like you.	**Sizden hoşlanıyorum.** seez·_dehn_ hohsh·lah·_nih_·yoh·room
I love you.	**Sizi seviyorum.** see·_zee_ seh·_vee_·yoh·room

► For formal and informal usage, see page 100.

Making Plans ───────────────

Would you like to...?	**...ister misiniz?** ...ees·_tehr_ mee·see·neez
– go out for coffee	– **Kahve içmeye gitmek** kah·_veh_ eech·meh·_yeh_ geet·_mehk_
– go for a drink	– **İçki içmeye gitmek** eech·_kee_ eech·meh·yeh geet·_mehk_

– go for a meal	**– Yemeğe çıkmak** yeh·<u>meh</u>·yeh chihk·<u>mahk</u>
What are your plans for...?	**...için planınız ne?** ...ee·<u>cheen</u> plah·nih·nihz <u>neh</u>
– tonight	**– Bu gece** boo geh·<u>jeh</u>
– tomorrow	**– Yarın** <u>yah</u>·rihn
– this weekend	**– Bu haftasonu** boo hahf·<u>tah</u>·soh·noo
Where would you like to go?	**Nereye gitmek istersiniz?** <u>neh</u>·reh·yeh geet·<u>mehk</u> ees·<u>tehr</u>·see·<u>neez</u>
I'd like to go to...	**...gitmek isterim.** ...geet·<u>mehk</u> ees·<u>teh</u>·reem
Do you like...?	**...ister misiniz?** ...ees·<u>tehr</u> mee·see·neez
Can I have your number/e-mail?	***Numaranızı/ Posta adresinizi* alabilir miyim?** noo·<u>mah</u>·rah·nih·<u>zih</u>/pohs·<u>tah</u> ahd·reh·see·nee·<u>zee</u> ah·lah·bee·<u>leer</u> mee·yeem

▶ For e-mail and phone, see page 47.

Pick-up [Chat-up] Lines

Can I join you?	**Size katılabilir miyim?** see·<u>zeh</u> kah·tih·lah·bee·<u>leer</u> mee·yeem
You're very attractive!	**Çok iyi görünüyorsunuz!** chohk ee·<u>yee</u> gur·ryu·<u>nyu</u>·yohr·soo·nooz
Shall we go somewhere quieter?	**Daha sakin bir yere gidelim mi?** dah·<u>hah</u> sah·<u>keen</u> beer yeh·reh gee·deh·<u>leem</u> mee

Accepting and Rejecting

Thank you. I'd love to.	**Teşekkür ederim. Sevinirim.** teh·shehk·<u>kyur</u> eh·deh·reem seh·vee·<u>nee</u>·reem
Where shall we meet?	**Nerede buluşalım?** neh·reh·deh boo·loo·<u>shah</u>·lihm
I'll meet you at *the bar/your hotel*.	**Sizi *barda/ otelinizde* bulurum.** see·<u>zee</u> bahr·<u>dah</u>/oh·teh·lee·neez·<u>deh</u> boo·loo·room
I'll come by at...	**...uğrarım.** ...oo·<u>rah</u>·rihm

▶ For time, see page 171.

What's your address?	**Adresin nedir?** ahd·reh·<u>seen</u> neh·deer
Thank you, but I'm busy.	**Teşekkür ederim ama meşgulüm.** teh·shehk·<u>kyur</u> eh·deh·reem ah·<u>mah</u> mehsh·<u>goo</u>·lyum
I'm not interested.	**İlgilenmiyorum.** eel·gee·<u>lehn</u>·mee·yoh·room
Leave me alone!	**Beni yalnız bırakın lütfen!** beh·<u>nee</u> yahl·<u>nihz</u> bih·<u>rah</u>·kihn <u>lyut</u>·fehn
Stop bothering me!	**Canımı sıkmayı kesin!** jah·nih·<u>mih</u> sihk·mah·<u>yih</u> <u>keh</u>·seen

Getting Physical

Can I *hug/kiss* you?	**Sizi *kucaklayabilir/ öpebilir* miyim?** see·<u>zee</u> koo·jahk·lah·yah·bee·<u>leer</u>/ur·peh·bee·<u>leer</u> mee·yeem
Yes.	**Evet.** <u>eh</u>·veht
No.	**Hayır.** <u>hah</u>·yihr
Stop!	**Dur!** door

Sexual Preferences

Are you gay?	**Gey misiniz?** <u>gay</u> mee·see·neez
I'm heterosexual.	**Ben karşı cinse ilgi duyarım.** behn kahr·<u>shih</u> jeen·<u>seh</u> eel·<u>gee</u> doo·<u>yah</u>·rihm
I'm homosexual.	**Eşcinselim.** ehsh·jeen·<u>seh</u>·leem
I'm bisexual.	**Biseksüelim.** beeh·sehk·syu·<u>eh</u>·leem
Do you like *men/ women*?	***Erkeklerden/ Kadınlardan* hoşlanır mısınız?** ehr·kehk·lehr·<u>dehn</u>/kah·dihn·lahr·<u>dahn</u> <u>hosh</u>·lah·<u>nihr</u> mih·sih·nihz

▼ Fun

Sightseeing

Essential

Where's the tourist office?	**Turist danışma bürosu nerede?** too·<u>reest</u> dah·nihsh·<u>mah</u> byu·roh·soo <u>neh</u>·reh·deh
What are the main points of interest?	**Başlıca ilginç yerler nelerdir?** bahsh·<u>lih</u>·jah eel·geench yehr·<u>lehr</u> neh·<u>lehr</u>·deer
Do you have tours in English?	**İngilizce turlarınız var mı?** een·geh·<u>leez</u>·jeh toor·lah·rih·<u>nihz</u> <u>vahr</u> mih
Can I have a *map/guide*?	***Harita/ Rehber** alabilir miyim?* hah·<u>ree</u>·tah/ reh·<u>ber</u> ah·lah·bee·<u>leer</u> mee·yeem

Tourist Information Office

Do you have any information on...?	**...hakkında bir bilginiz var mı?** ... hahk·kihn·<u>dah</u> beer beel·gee·<u>neez</u> <u>vahr</u> mih
Can you recommend...?	**...önerebilir misiniz?** ...ur·neh·reh·bee·<u>leer</u> mee·see·neez
– a boat trip	**– Bir gemi gezisi** beer geh·<u>mee</u> geh·zee·see
– an excursion	**– Bir gezinti** beer geh·zeen·<u>tee</u>
– a sightseeing tour	**– Bir tur** beer toor

Turizm Danışma Bürosu (tourist information offices) are located in cities throughout Turkey. In smaller cities, the office is often located in or near the main square. Big cities usually have several offices. The tourist office can provide maps and information about the area and help in making reservations. Travel agents are also helpful in assisting with information and can often offer good rates on hotel reservations.

Tours

I'd like to go on the tour to...	**...turla gitmek istiyorum.** ...<u>toor</u>·lah geet·<u>mehk</u> ees·<u>tee</u>·yoh·room
When's the next tour?	**Bir sonraki tur ne zaman?** beer <u>sohn</u>·rah·kee toor <u>neh</u> zah·mahn
Are there tours in English?	**İngilizce turlar var mı?** een·gee·<u>leez</u>·jeh toor·<u>lahr</u> <u>vahr</u> mih
Is there an English-speaking guide?	**İngilizce konuşan bir rehber var mı?** een·gee·<u>leez</u>·jeh koh·noo·<u>shahn</u> beer reh·<u>behr</u> <u>vahr</u> mih
What time do we *leave/return*?	**Saat kaçta *ayrılacağız/ döneceğiz*?** sah·<u>aht</u> kahch·<u>tah</u> *ie·rih·lah·<u>jah</u>·ihz/ dur·neh·<u>jeh</u>·eez*
We'd like to have a look at the...	**...bakmak istiyoruz.** ...bahk·<u>mahk</u> ees·<u>tee</u>·yoh·rooz
Can we stop here...?	**Burada...durabilir miyiz?** <u>boo</u>·rah·dah... doo·rah·bee·<u>leer</u> mee·yeez
– to take photographs	**– fotoğraf çekmek için** foh·toh·<u>rahf</u> chehk·<u>mehk</u> ee·<u>cheen</u>
– for souvenirs	**– hediyelik eşya satın almak için** heh·dee·yeh·<u>leek</u> ehsh·<u>yah</u> sah·<u>tihn</u> ahl·<u>mahk</u> ee·cheen
– to use the restroom [toilet]	**– tuvalete gitmek için** too·vah·leh·<u>teh</u> geet·<u>mehk</u> ee·<u>cheen</u>
Is there access for the disabled?	**Özürlüler girebilir mi?** ur·zyur·lyu·<u>lehr</u> gee·reh·bee·<u>leer</u> mee

▶ For ticketing, see page 18.

Sights

Where is...? | ...**nerede?** ...<u>neh</u>·reh·deh

- the battleground — **Muharebe meydanı** moo·hah·reh·<u>beh</u> may·dah·nih
- the botanical garden — **Botanik bahçesi** boh·tah·<u>neek</u> bah·cheh·<u>see</u>
- the castle — **Kale** kah·<u>leh</u>
- the downtown area — **Kent merkezi** kehnt mehr·keh·<u>zee</u>
- the fountain — **Çeşme** chehsh·<u>meh</u>
- the library — **Kütüphane** kyu·tyup·hah·<u>neh</u>
- the market — **Pazar** pah·<u>zahr</u>
- the museum — **Müze** myu·<u>zeh</u>
- the old town — **Eski kent** ehs·<u>kee</u> kehnt
- the palace — **Saray** sah·<u>rie</u>
- the park — **Park** pahrk

111

Where is...?	...**nerede?** ...neh·reh·deh
- the shopping area	- **Alış veriş merkezi** ah·lihsh veh·reesh mehr·keh·zee
- the town square	- **Kasaba meydanı** kah·sah·bah may·dah·nih
Can you show me on the map?	**Bana haritada gösterebilir misiniz?** bah·nah hah·ree·tah·dah gurs·teh·reh·bee·leer mee·see·neez

▶ For directions, see page 33.

Impressions

It's...	...**-dir.** ...deer
- amazing	- **Hayret verici** hie·reht veh·ree·jee
- beautiful	- **Güzel** gyu·zehl
- boring	- **Sıkıcı** sih·kih·jih
- interesting	- **İlginç** eel·ginch
- magnificent	- **Muhteşem** mooh·teh·shehm
- romantic	- **Romantik** roh·mahn·teek
- strange	- **Şaşırtıcı** shah·shihr·tih·jih
- stunning	- **Çarpıcı** chahr·pih·jih
- terrible	- **Berbat** behr·baht
- ugly	- **Çirkin** cheer·keen
I like it.	**Beğendim.** beh·yehn·deem
I don't like it.	**Beğenmedim.** beh·yehn·meh·deem

Religion

Where's...?	...**nerede?** ...neh·reh·deh
- the cathedral	- **Katedral** kah·tehd·rahl

– the *Catholic/ Protestant* church	– *Katolik/ Protestan* kilisesi kah·toh·<u>leek</u>/ proh·tehs·<u>tahn</u> kee·lee·seh·<u>see</u>
– the mosque	– **Cami** jah·<u>mee</u>
– the shrine	– **Mabet** mah·<u>baht</u>
– the synagogue	– **Havra** <u>hahv</u>·rah
– the temple	– **Tapınak** tah·pih·<u>nahk</u>
What time is *mass/ the service*?	*Ayin/İbadet* saat kaçta? ah·<u>yihn</u>/ ee·bah·<u>deht</u> sah·<u>aht</u> kahch·<u>tah</u>

Today Turkey is a Muslim country and the majority of the population belongs to the Sunni branch of Islam. It is, however, a secular state. Individuals are guaranteed freedom of religion by the constitution, which at the same time protects religious groups. The constitution also specifies that the political system must be explicitly religion-free. That means religious groups may not form political parties or establish schools based on a particular faith. Turkey also prohibits wearing religious garments, such as head covers, in all government buildings as well as schools and universities.

Shopping

Essential

Where is the *market/mall [shopping centre]*?	*Market/ Alış veriş merkezi* nerede? mahr·<u>keht</u>/ah·<u>lihsh</u> veh·<u>reesh</u> mehr·keh·<u>zee</u> <u>neh</u>·reh·deh
I'm just looking.	**Sadece bakıyorum.** <u>sah</u>·deh·jeh bah·<u>kih</u>·yoh·room
Can you help me?	**Bana yardım edebilir misiniz?** bah·nah yahr·<u>dihm</u> eh·deh·bee·<u>leer</u> mee·see·neez

I'm being helped.	**Yardım alıyorum.** yahr·<u>dihm</u> ah·<u>lih</u>·yoh·room
How much?	**Ne kadar?** <u>neh</u> kah·dahr
That one.	**Şunu.** shoo·<u>noo</u>
That's all, thanks.	**Hepsi bu, teşekkürler.** <u>hehp</u>·see boo teh·shehk·kyur·<u>lehr</u>
Where do I pay?	**Nereye ödeyeceğim?** <u>neh</u>·reh·yeh ur·deh·yeh·<u>jeh</u>·yeem
I'll pay in *cash/by credit card*.	***Nakit/ Kredi kartı* ile ödeyeceğim.** *nah·<u>keet</u>/ kreh·<u>dee</u> kahr·tih ee·leh ur·deh·yeh·jeh·yeem*
A receipt, please.	**Fatura lütfen.** <u>fah</u>·too·rah <u>lyut</u>·fehn

---

> *i*
>
> One thing not to miss while in Turkey is the weekly **pazar** (neighborhood market), found outside in almost every town throughout the country. In Istanbul, be sure to visit the **Kapali Çarşı** (Covered market or Grand Bazaar), the **Mısır Çarşısı** (Spice Market) and the **Balık Pazarı** (Fish Bazaar). Beware of pickpockets though. They are prevalent in these places, so tourists should pay attention their valuables.

Stores

Where is...?	**...nerede?** ...<u>neh</u>·reh·deh
– the antique store	**– Antikacı** ahn·<u>tee</u>·kah·jih
– the bakery	**– Fırın** fih·<u>rihn</u>
– the bank	**– Banka** bahn·<u>kah</u>
– the bookstore	**– Kitapçı** kee·tahp·<u>chih</u>
– the clothing store	**– Elbise mağazası** ehl·<u>bee</u>·seh mah·<u>ah</u>·zah·sih
– the delicatessen	**– Şarküteri** shahr·kyu·teh·<u>ree</u>

– the department store	– **Mağaza** mah·<u>ah</u>·zah
– the gift shop	– **Hediyelik eşya dükkanı** heh·dee·yeh·<u>leek</u> ehsh·<u>yah</u> dyuk·<u>kah</u>·nih
– the health food store	– **Sağlıklı yiyecekler dükkanı** sah·lihk·<u>lih</u> yee·yeh·jehk·<u>lehr</u> dyuk·kah·<u>nih</u>

Where is...?	...nerede? ...<u>neh</u>·reh·deh
– the jeweler	– **Kuyumcu** koo·yoom·<u>joo</u>
– the liquor store [off-licence]	– **Tekel bayii** teh·<u>kehl</u> bah·yee·<u>ee</u>
– the market	– **Market** mahr·<u>keht</u>
– the pastry shop	– **Pastane** pahs·tah·<u>neh</u>
– the pharmacy [chemist]	– **Eczane** ehj·zah·<u>neh</u>
– the produce [grocery] store	– **Manav** mah·<u>nahv</u>
– the shoe store	– **Ayakkabıcı** ah·<u>yahk</u>·kah·bih·jih
– the shopping mall [centre]	– **Alış veriş merkezi** ah·<u>lihsh</u> veh·<u>reesh</u> mehr·keh·<u>zee</u>
– the souvenir store	– **Hediyelik eşya dükkanı** heh·dee·yeh·<u>leek</u> ehsh·<u>yah</u> dyuk·kah·nih
– the supermarket	– **Süpermarket** syu·<u>pehr</u>·mahr·keht
– the tobacconist	– **Tütüncü** tyu·tyun·<u>jyu</u>
– the toy store	– **Oyuncakçı** oh·yoon·jahk·<u>chih</u>

Services

Can you recommend...?	...önerebilir misiniz? ...ur·neh·reh·bee·<u>leer</u> mee·see·neez
– a barber	– **Berber** behr·behr
– a dry cleaner	– **Kuru temizleyici** koo·<u>roo</u> teh·meez·leh·yee·<u>jee</u>
– a hairdresser	– **Kuaför** koo·ah·<u>furr</u>
– a laundromat [launderette]	– **Çamaşırhane** chah·mah·shihr·hah·<u>neh</u>

– a nail salon	– **Güzellik salonu** gyu·zehl·<u>leek</u> sah·loh·<u>noo</u>
– a spa	– **Kaplıca** <u>kahp</u>·lih·jah
– a travel agency	– **Seyahat acentası** seh·yah·<u>haht</u> ah·jehn·tah·<u>sih</u>
Can you...this?	**Bunu...misiniz?** boo·<u>noo</u>...mee·see·neez
– alter	– **değiştirebilir** deh·yeesh·tee·reh·bee·<u>leer</u>
– clean	– **temizleyebilir** teh·meez·leh·yeh·bee·<u>leer</u>
– mend	– **yamalayabilir** yah·mah·lah·yah·bee·<u>leer</u>
– press	– **ütüleyebilir** yu·tyu·leh·yeh·bee·<u>leer</u>
When will it be ready?	**Ne zaman hazır olacak?** neh zah·<u>mahn</u> hah·<u>zihr</u> oh·lah·<u>jahk</u>

Spa

I'd like...	**...istiyorum.** ...ees·<u>tee</u>·yoh·room
– an *eyebrow/ bikini wax*	– **Kaş aldırma/Ağda** <u>kahsh</u> ahl·dih·mah/ **ah**·<u>dah</u>
– a facial	– **Yüz masajı** yyuz mah·sah·<u>jih</u>
– a *manicure/ pedicure*	– **Manikür/Pedikür** mah·nee·<u>kyur</u>/ peh·dee·<u>kyur</u>
– a (sports) massage	– **Bir (spor) masajı** beer (spohr) mah·sah·<u>jih</u>
Do you do...?	**...yapar mısınız?** ...yah·<u>pahr</u> mih·sih·nihz
– acupuncture	– **Akupunktur** ah·koo·poonk·<u>toor</u>
– aromatherapy	– **Aroma terapi** ah·<u>roh</u>·mah teh·rah·<u>pee</u>
– oxygen treatment	– **Oksijen tedavisi** ohk·see·<u>jehn</u> teh·dah·vee·<u>see</u>
Is there a sauna?	**Sauna var mı?** sah·oo·<u>nah</u> <u>vahr</u> mih

i

Turkey is an excellent destination for visiting spas. There are many throughout the country and are recommended by the Turks as a means of natural therapy or a cure for certain ailments. There are many different treatments to enjoy: bathing in thermal springs, mud baths, wraps, massages and, the most famous of all, the Turkish bath. Turkish baths are a type of wet sauna or steam bath and have been known in Turkey for centuries. The concept was only exported to Europe around the mid-1800s.

If you are looking for a unique experience, consider visiting the hot springs in Kangal, located in the Sivas province, in Central Anatolia. In this thermal bath, mineral water flows in from five different springs and along with it so do innumerable small fish (small meaning about 1 to 5 inches long). Bathing with them is said to cure many skin illnesses.

Hair Salon

I'd like...	**...istiyorum.** ...ees·<u>tee</u>·yoh·room
– an appointment for *today/ tomorrow*	– *Bugün/ Yarın için bir randevu* <u>boo</u>·gyun/ <u>yah</u>·rihn ee·cheen beer <u>rahn</u>·deh·<u>voo</u>
– some color	– **Boyama** boh·yah·<u>mah</u>
– some highlights	– **Röfle** rurf·<u>leh</u>
– my hair styled	– **Saç şekillendirme** <u>sahch</u> sheh·keel·lehn·deer·<u>meh</u>
– a haircut	– **Kestirmek** kehs·teer·<u>mehk</u>
– a trim	– **Uçlarından aldırmak** ooch·lah·rihn·<u>dahn</u> ahl·dihr·<u>mahk</u>
Don't cut it too short.	**Çok kısa kesmeyin.** chohk kih·<u>sah</u> <u>kehs</u>·meh·yeen
Shorter here.	**Burayı kısaltın.** boo·rah·<u>yih</u> kih·<u>sahl</u>·tihn

Sales Help

When does the...*open/close*?	**...ne zaman *açılıyor/ kapanıyor*?** ...neh zah-<u>mahn</u> ah-chih-<u>lih</u>-yohr/kah-pah-nih-yohr
Where is...?	**...nerede?** ...<u>neh</u>·reh·deh
– the cashier [cash desk]	– **Kasa** kah·<u>sah</u>
– the escalator	– **Yürüyen merdiven** yyu·ryu·<u>yehn</u> mehr·dee·<u>vehn</u>
– the elevator [lift]	– **Asansör** ah·sahn·<u>surr</u>
– the fitting room	– **Giyinme kabinleri** gee·yeen·<u>meh</u> kah·been·leh·<u>ree</u>
– the store directory [guide]	– **Mağaza rehberi** mah·<u>ah</u>·zah rehh·beh·ree
Can you help me?	**Bana yardım edebilir misiniz?** bah·nah yahr·<u>dihm</u> eh·deh·bee·<u>leer</u> mee·see·neez
I'm just looking.	**Sadece bakıyorum.** <u>sah</u>·deh·jeh bah·<u>kih</u>·yoh·room
I'm being helped.	**Yardım alıyorum.** yahr·<u>dihm</u> ah·<u>lih</u>·yoh·room
Do you have any...?	**...var mı?** ...<u>vahr</u> mih
Can you show me...?	**...gösterebilir misiniz?** ...gurs·teh·reh·bee·<u>leer</u> mee·see·neez
Can you *ship/wrap* it?	***Kargoyla yollayabilir/ Paketleyebilir* misiniz?** kahr·<u>gohy</u>·lah yohl·lah·yah·bee·<u>leer</u>/ pah·<u>keht</u>·leh·yeh·bee·<u>leer</u> mee·see·neez
How much?	**Ne kadar?** <u>neh</u> kah·dahr
That's all, thanks.	**Hepsi bu, teşekkürler.** hehp·see <u>boo</u> teh·shehk·<u>kyur</u>·lehr

▶ For clothing items, see page 127.

▶ For food items, see page 84.

▶ For souvenirs, see page 122.

You May Hear...

Yardımcı olabilir miyim? yahr·dihm·<u>jih</u>
oh·lah·bee·<u>leer</u> mee·yeem

Can I help you?

Bir dakika. beer dah·<u>kee</u>·kah

One moment.

Ne istersiniz? <u>neh</u> ees·<u>tehr</u>·see·neez

What would you
like?

Başka bir şey? bahsh·<u>kah</u> beer <u>shay</u>

Anything else?

Preferences

I'd like something...	**...bir şey istiyorum.** ...beer <u>shay</u> ees·<u>tee</u>·yoh·room
– cheap/expensive	– **Ucuz/Pahalı** oo·<u>jooz</u>/pah·<u>hah</u>·lih
– larger/smaller	– **Daha *büyük/küçük*** dah·<u>hah</u> byu·<u>yyuk</u>/ kyu·<u>chyuk</u>
– from this region	– **Bu çevreden** boo chehv·reh·<u>dehn</u>
Is it real?	**Hakiki mi?** hah·kee·<u>kee</u> mee
Could you show me *this/that*?	***Bunu/Onu* bana gösterebilir misiniz?** boo·<u>noo</u>/oh·<u>noo</u> bah·nah gyus·teh·reh·bee·<u>leer</u> mee·see·neez

Decisions

That's not quite what I want.	**Bu tam istediğim gibi değil.** boo <u>tahm</u> ees·teh·dee·<u>yeem</u> gee·bee <u>deh</u>·yeel
I don't like it.	**Beğenmedim.** beh·<u>yehn</u>·meh·deem
That's too expensive.	**Çok pahalı.** chohk pah·<u>hah</u>·lih
I'd like to think about it.	**Biraz düşünmek istiyorum.** <u>bee</u>·rahz dyu·shyun·<u>mehk</u> ees·<u>tee</u>·yoh·room

I'll take it. **Alıyorum.** ah·<u>lih</u>·yoh·room

Bargaining

That's too much.	**Çok pahalı.** <u>chohk</u> pah·hah·<u>lih</u>
I'll give you...	**...veririm.** ...veh·<u>ree</u>·reem
I only have...lira.	**Sadece...liram var.** <u>sah</u>·deh·jeh...lee·<u>rahm</u> vahr
Is that your best price?	**En son fiyat bu mu?** ehn sohn fee·<u>yaht</u> <u>boo</u> moo
Give me a discount.	**Bana bir indirim yapın.** bah·<u>nah</u> beer een·deer·<u>reem</u> yah·pihn

▶ For numbers, see page 169.

Paying

How much?	**Ne kadar?** <u>neh</u> kah·dahr
I'll pay by...	**...ile ödeyeceğim.** ...ee·<u>leh</u> ur·deh·yeh·<u>jeh</u>·yeem
– in cash	**– Nakit** nah·<u>keet</u>
– by credit card	**– Kredi kartı ile** kreh·<u>dee</u> kahr·<u>tih</u> ee·leh
– by traveler's check [cheque]	**– Seyahat çeki** seh·yah·<u>haht</u> cheh·<u>kee</u>
A receipt, please.	**Fatura lütfen.** fah·<u>too</u>·rah <u>lyut</u>·fehn

Major credit cards are commonly accepted, though not everywhere. It is a good idea to have some cash on hand, just in case. Note that some establishments also pass on the credit-processing costs, usually between 3–6%, as a surcharge.

You May Hear...

Nasıl ödeyeceksiniz? nah·<u>sihl</u> ur·deh·yeh·<u>jehk</u>·see·neez

How are you paying?

İşlem *onaylanmadı/ kabul edilmedi*. eesh·<u>lehm</u> oh·nie·<u>lahn</u>·mah·dih/kah·<u>bool</u> eh·<u>deel</u>·meh·dee

This transaction has not been *approved/ accepted*.

Başka bir kimlik kartınızı görebilir miyim? bahsh·<u>kah</u> beer keem·<u>leek</u> kahr·tih·nih·<u>zih</u> gur·reh·bee·<u>leer</u> mee·yeem

May I see another ID card?

Sadece nakit lütfen. <u>sah</u>·deh·jeh nah·<u>keet</u> <u>lyut</u>·fehn

Cash only, please.

Bozuğunuz yok mu? boh·zoo·**oo**·<u>nooz</u> <u>yohk</u> moo

Do you have any smaller change?

Complaints

I'd like...	**...istiyorum.** ...ees·<u>tee</u>·yoh·room
– to exchange this	– **Bunu değiştirmek** boo·<u>noo</u> deh·yeesh·teer·<u>mehk</u>
– to return this	– **Geri vermek** geh·<u>ree</u> vehr·<u>mehk</u>
– a refund	– **Paramı geri** pah·rah·<u>mih</u> geh·<u>ree</u>
– to see the manager	– **Müdürü görmek** myu·dyu·<u>ryu</u> gurr·<u>mehk</u>

Souvenirs

bottle of wine	**bir şişe şarap** beer shee·<u>sheh</u> shah·<u>rahp</u>
box of chocolates	**kutu çikolata** koo·<u>too</u> chee·koh·<u>lah</u>·tah
calendar	**takvim** tahk·<u>veem</u>

carpets	**halı** hah·<u>lih</u>
dolls	**bebek** beh·<u>behk</u>
jewelry	**mücevher** myu·jehv·<u>hehr</u>
key ring	**anahtarlık** ah·nahh·tahr·<u>lihk</u>
lace	**dantel** dahn·<u>tehl</u>
leather goods	**deri eşyalar** deh·<u>ree</u> ehsh·yah·<u>lahr</u>
perfume	**parfüm** pahr·<u>fyum</u>
porcelain	**porselen** pohr·seh·<u>lehn</u>
postcards	**kartpostal** kahrt·pohs·<u>tahl</u>
pottery	**çömlek** churm·<u>lehk</u>
rug	**kilim** kee·<u>leem</u>
scarf	**eşarp** eh·<u>shahrp</u>
silk garments	**ipek eşya** ee·<u>pehk</u> ehsh·<u>yah</u>
souvenir guide	**hediyelik eşya rehberi** heh·dee·yeh·<u>leek</u> ehsh·<u>yah</u> reh·beh·<u>ree</u>
T-shirt	**tişört** tee·<u>shurrt</u>
tea towel	**kurulama bezi** koo·roo·lah·<u>mah</u> beh·<u>zee</u>
Can I see *this/ that*?	*Buna/ Şuna bakabilir miyim?* boo·<u>nah</u>/ shoo·<u>nah</u> bah·kah·bee·<u>leer</u> mee·yeem
It's the one in the *window/display case*.	**Vitrindeki./Sergilenen.** veet·reen·deh·<u>kee</u>/ sehr·gee·leh·<u>nehn</u>
I'd like...	**...istiyorum.** ...ees·<u>tee</u>·yoh·room
- a battery	**- Pil** peel
- a bracelet	**- Bilezik** bee·leh·<u>zeek</u>
- a brooch	**- Broş** brohsh

– earrings	– **Küpe** kyu·<u>peh</u>
– a necklace	– **Kolye** kohl·<u>yeh</u>
– a ring	– **Yüzük** yyu·<u>zyuk</u>
– a watch	– **Kol saati** <u>kohl</u> sah·ah·<u>tee</u>
– copper	– **Bakır** bah·<u>kihr</u>
– crystal	– **Kuartz** koo·<u>ahrtz</u>
– diamond	– **Elmas** ehl·<u>mahs</u>
– *white/yellow* gold	– ***Beyaz/Sarı** altın* beh·<u>yahz</u>/sah·<u>rih</u> ahl·<u>tihn</u>
– pearl	– **İnci** een·<u>jee</u>

124

- pewter	**Kurşun-kalay alaşımı** koor·<u>shoon</u> kah·<u>lie</u> ah·lah·shih·<u>mih</u>
- platinum	**Platin** plah·<u>teen</u>
- sterling silver	**Som gümüş** sohm gyu·<u>myush</u>
Is this real?	**Hakiki mi?** hah·kee·<u>kee</u> mee
Can you engrave it?	**İşleyebilir misin?** eesh·leh·yeh·bee·<u>leer</u> mee·seen

> For everything under one roof, be sure to go shopping in the **Kapali Çarsi** (covered market or Grand Bazaar) in Istanbul. One of the largest covered markets in the world, there are literally thousands of shops and restaurants selling just about anything imaginable. Here you'll be able to find lots of Turkish souvenirs to take back home with you and it's a great chance to practice your haggling skills! Be sure to enjoy the ambiance, but stay alert for pickpockets and bag snatchers.

Antiques

How old is this?	**Bu ne kadar eski?** boo <u>neh</u> kah·dahr ehs·<u>kee</u>
Will I have problems with customs?	**Gümrükte sorun çıkar mı?** gyum·ryuk·<u>teh</u> soh·<u>roon</u> chih·<u>kahr</u> mih
Is there a certificate of authenticity?	**Hakikilik belgesi var mı?** hah·<u>kee</u>·kee·leek behl·geh·<u>see</u> <u>vahr</u> mih

Clothing

I'd like...	**...istiyorum.** ...ees·<u>tee</u>·yoh·room
Can I try this on?	**Bunu deneyebilir miyim?** boo·<u>noo</u> deh·neh·yeh·bee·<u>leer</u> mee·yeem
It doesn't fit.	**Olmadı.** <u>ohl</u>·mah·dih

It's too...	Çok... chohk...
– big	– **büyük** byu·<u>yyuk</u>
– small	– **küçük** kyu·<u>chyuk</u>
– short	– **kısa** kih·<u>sah</u>
– long	– **uzun** oo·<u>zoon</u>
Do you have this in size...?	**Bunun...bedeni var mı?** boo·<u>noon</u>... beh·<u>deh</u>·nee vahr mih
Do you have this in a *bigger/smaller* size?	**Bunun daha *büyük/ küçük* bedeni var mı?** boo·<u>noon</u> dah·<u>hah</u> byu·<u>yyuk</u>/kyu·<u>chyuk</u> beh·deh·<u>nee</u> vahr mih

▶ For numbers, see page 169.

You May See...

ERKEK GİYİMİ	men's clothing
BAYAN GİYİMİ	women's clothing
ÇOCUK GİYİMİ	children's clothing

Color

I'm looking for something in...	**...bir şeyler arıyorum.** ...beer shay·lehr ah·<u>rih</u>·yoh·room
– beige	– **Bej** behj
– black	– **Siyah** see·<u>yah</u>
– blue	– **Mavi** mah·<u>vee</u>
– brown	– **Kahverengi** kah·<u>veh</u>·rehn·<u>gee</u>
– green	– **Yeşil** yeh·<u>sheel</u>
– gray	– **Gri** gree

– orange	**– Portakal rengi** pohr·tah·<u>kahl</u> rehn·gee
– pink	**– Pembe** pehm·<u>beh</u>
– purple	**– Mor** mohr
– red	**– Kırmızı** kihr·mih·<u>zih</u>
– white	**– Beyaz** beh·<u>yahz</u>
– yellow	**– Sarı** sah·<u>rih</u>

Clothes and Accessories

backpack	**sırt çantası** sihrt chahn·tah·<u>sih</u>
belt	**kemer** keh·<u>mehr</u>
bikini	**bikini** bee·<u>kee</u>·nee
blouse	**bluz** blooz
bra	**sütyen** syut·<u>yehn</u>
briefs [underpants]	**külot** kyu·<u>loht</u>
coat	**palto** pahl·<u>toh</u>
dress	**elbise** ehl·<u>bee</u>·seh
hat	**şapka** shahp·<u>kah</u>
jacket	**ceket** jeh·<u>keht</u>
jeans	**kot pantalon** koht pahn·tah·<u>lohn</u>
pajamas	**pijama** pee·<u>jah</u>·mah
pants [trousers]	**pantalon** pahn·tah·<u>lohn</u>
pantyhose [tights]	**tayt** tiet
purse [handbag]	**el çantası** ehl chahn·tah·<u>sih</u>
raincoat	**yağmurluk** <u>yah</u>·moor·look
scarf	**eşarp** eh·<u>shahrp</u>
shirt (men's)	**gömlek** gurm·<u>lehk</u>
shorts	**şort** shohrt

skirt	**etek** eh·tehk
socks	**çorap** choh·rahp
suit	**takım elbise** tah·kihm ehl·bee·seh
sunglasses	**güneş gözlüğü** gyu·nehsh gurz·lyu·yyu
sweater	**süveter** syu·veh·tehr
sweatshirt	**sweatshirt** sveht·shurrt
swimming trunks/ swimsuit	**mayo** mah·yoh
T-shirt	**tişört** tee·shurrt
tie	**kravat** krah·vaht
underwear	**külot** kyu·loht

Fabric

I'd like...	**...istiyorum.** ...ees·tee·yoh·room
– cotton	**– Pamuklu** pah·mook·loo
– denim	**– Kot kumaşı** koht koo·mah·shih
– lace	**– Dantel** dahn·tehl
– leather	**– Deri** deh·ree
– linen	**– Keten** keh·tehn
– silk	**– İpek** ee·pehk
– wool	**– Yün** yyun
Is it machine washable?	**Makinede yıkanabilir mi?** mah·kee·neh·deh yih·kah·nah·bee·leer mee

Shoes

I'd like...	**...istiyorum.** ...ees·tee·yoh·room
– *high-heeled/flat* shoes	**– *Yüksek topuklu/Düz taban* ayakkabı** *yyuk·sehk toh·pook·loo/dyuz tah·bahn* ah·yahk·kah·bih

– boots	– **Çizme** cheez·meh
– loafers	– **Mokasen** moh·kah·sehn
– sandals	– **Sandalet** sahn·dah·leht
– shoes	– **Ayakkabı** ah·yahk·kah·bih
– slippers	– **Terlik** tehr·leek
– sneakers	– **Koşu ayakkabısı** koh·shoo ah·yahk·kah·bih·sih
In size...	**...numara.** ...noo·mah·rah

▶ For numbers, see page 169.

Sizes

small	**küçük** kyu·chyuk
medium	**orta** ohr·tah
large	**büyük** byu·yyuk
extra large	**çok büyük** chohk byu·yyuk
petite	**ufak** oo·fahk
plus size	**battal boy** baht·tahl boy

Newsstand and Tobacconist ─────────

Do you sell English-language *books/ newspapers*?	**İngilizce *kitap/ gazete* satıyor musunuz?** een·gee·leez·jeh *kee·tahp/gah·zeh·teh* sah·tih·yohr moo·soo·nooz
I'd like...	**...istiyorum.** ...ees·tee·yoh·room
– candy [sweets]	– **Şeker** sheh·kehr
– chewing gum	– **Sakız** sah·kihz
– a chocolate bar	– **Çikolata** chee·koh·lah·tah

– cigars	**– Puro** poo·<u>roh</u>
– *a pack/carton of* cigarettes	**– *Paket/Karton* sigara** pah·<u>keht</u>/cahr·<u>tohn</u> see·gah·<u>rah</u>
– a lighter	**– Çakmak** chahk·<u>mahk</u>
– a magazine	**– Dergi** dehr·<u>gee</u>
– matches	**– Kibrit** keeb·<u>reet</u>
– a newspaper	**– Gazete** gah·<u>zeh</u>·teh
– *a road/town* map of...	**– ...*yol/ kent* haritası** ...*yohl/kehnt* hah·ree·tah·<u>sih</u>
– stamps	**– Pul** pool

Photography

I'm looking for...camera.	**...bir fotoğraf makinesi arıyorum.** ...beer foh·**toh**·<u>rahf</u> mah·<u>kee</u>·neh·see ah·<u>rih</u>·yoh·room
– an automatic	**– Otomatik** oh·toh·mah·<u>teek</u>
– a digital	**– Dijital** dee·jee·<u>tahl</u>
– a disposable	**– Tek kullanımlık** <u>tehk</u> kool·<u>lah</u>·nihm·lihk
I'd like...	**...istiyorum.** ...ees·<u>tee</u>·yoh·room
– a battery	**– Pil** peel
– digital prints	**– Dijital baskı** dee·jee·<u>tahl</u> bahs·<u>kih</u>
– a memory card	**– Hafıza kartı** hah·fih·<u>zah</u> kahr·<u>tih</u>
Can I print digital photos here?	**Dijital fotoğrafları burda basabilir miyim?** dee·jee·<u>tahl</u> foh·toh·<u>rahf</u>·lah·rih boor·dah bah·sah·bee·<u>leer</u> mee·yeem

130

Sports and Leisure

Essential

When's the game?	**Maç kaçta?** mahch kahch·tah
Where's...?	**...nerede?** ...neh·reh·deh
– the beach	**– Plaj** plahj
– the park	**– Park** pahrk
– the pool	**– Yüzme havuzu** yyuz·meh hah·voo·zoo
Is it safe to *swim/ dive* here?	**Burada *yüzmek/dalmak* güvenli mi?** boo·rah·dah yyuz·mehk/dahl·mahk gyu·vehn·lee mee
Can I rent [hire] golf clubs?	**Golf sopalarını kiralayabilir miyim?** gohlf soh·pah·lah·rih·nih kee·rah·lah·yah·bee·leer mee·yeem
How much per hour?	**Saatlik ücreti nedir?** sah·aht·leek yuj·reh·tee neh·deer
How far is it to...?	**...buradan ne kadar uzakta?** ...boo·rah·dahn neh kah·dahr oo·zahk·tah
Can you show me on the map?	**Bana haritada gösterebilir misiniz?** bah·nah hah·ree·tah·dah gurs·teh·reh·bee·leer mee·see·neez

Spectator Sports

When's...?	**...ne zaman?** ...neh zah·mahn
– the basketball game	**– Basketbol maçı** bahs·keht·bohl mah·chih
– the boxing match	**– Boks maçı** bohks mah·chih
– the cycling race	**– Bisiklet yarışı** bee·seek·leht yah·rih·shih

– the golf tournament	– **Golf turnuvası** gohlf toor·noo·vah·<u>sih</u>
– the soccer [football] game	– **Futbol maçı** <u>foot</u>·bohl mah·chih
– the tennis match	– **Tenis maçı** teh·<u>nees</u> mah·chih
– the volleyball game	– **Voleybol maçı** <u>voh</u>·lay·bohl mah·chih
Which teams are playing?	**Hangi takımlar oynuyor?** <u>hahn</u>·gee tah·kihm·<u>lahr</u> oy·<u>noo</u>·yohr
Where's...?	**...nerede?** ...<u>neh</u>·reh·deh
– the horsetrack	– **At yarışı** aht yah·rih·<u>shih</u>
– the racetrack	– **Hipodrom** hee·pohd·rohm
– the stadium	– **Stadyum** <u>stah</u>·dyoom
Where can I place a bet?	**Nerede bahis oynayabilirim?** <u>neh</u>·reh·deh bah·<u>hees</u> oy·nah·yah·bee·<u>lee</u>·reem

i Since Turkey is surrounded by so much water, it is no surprise that water sports are popular. Swimming, sailing, scuba diving and windsurfing are common in the seas, while one can go rafting or canoeing on one of Turkey's many rivers. Other sports like caving and trekking can be enjoyed in addition to golf or horseback riding. The national sports, however, are soccer and wrestling. Oil wrestling has in fact been practiced since Ottoman times.

Participating

Where's...?	**...nerede?** ...<u>neh</u>·reh·deh
– the golf course	– **Golf sahası** <u>gohlf</u> sah·hah·sih
– the gym	– **Spor klübü** <u>spohr</u> klyu·byu

– the park	**– Park** pahrk
– the tennis courts	**– Tenis kortları** teh·<u>nees</u> kohrt·lah·rih
How much per...?	**...ücreti nedir?** ...yuj·reh·<u>tee</u> <u>neh</u>·deer
– day	**– Günlük** gyun·<u>lyuk</u>
– hour	**– Saatlik** sah·aht·<u>leek</u>
– game	**– Bir oyun** beer oh·<u>yoon</u>
– round	**– Bir tur** beer toor
Can I rent [hire]...?	**...kiralayabilir miyim?** ... kee·rah·lah·yah·bee·<u>leer</u> mee·yeem
– golf clubs	**– Sopa** soh·<u>pah</u>
– equipment	**– Donanım** doh·nah·<u>nihm</u>
– a racket	**– Raket** rah·<u>keht</u>

At the Beach/Pool

Where's the *beach/ pool*?	***Plaj/Havuz nerede?*** plahj/hah·<u>vooz</u> <u>neh</u>·reh·deh
Is there...?	***Burada...var mı?*** <u>boo</u>·rah·dah...<u>vahr</u> mih
– a kiddie [paddling] pool	– **çocuk havuzu** choh·<u>jook</u> hah·voo·zoo
– an *indoor/ outdoor* pool	– ***kapalı/açık havuz*** kah·pah·<u>lih</u>/ah·<u>chihk</u> hah·<u>vooz</u>
– a lifeguard	– **cankurtaran** jan·<u>koor</u>·tah·rahn
Is it safe...?	***...güvenli mi?*** ...gyu·vehn·<u>lee</u> mee
– to swim	– **Yüzmek** yyuz·<u>mehk</u>
– to dive	– **Dalmak** dahl·<u>mahk</u>
– for children	– **Çocuklar için** choh·<u>jook</u>·lahr ee·cheen

▶ For travel with children, see page 145.

I want to rent [hire]...	***...Kiralamak istiyorum.*** ...kee·rah·lah·<u>mahk</u> ees·<u>tee</u>·yoh·room
– a deck chair	– **Katlanabilir koltuk** kaht·lah·nah·bee·<u>leer</u> kohl·<u>took</u>
– diving equipment	– **Dalış donanımı** dah·<u>lihsh</u> doh·<u>nah</u>·nih·mih
– a jet-ski	– **Jet ski** jeht skee
– a motorboat	– **Deniz motoru** deh·<u>neez</u> moh·toh·<u>roo</u>
– a rowboat	– **Sandal** sahn·<u>dahl</u>
– snorkeling equipment	– **Şnorkel takımı** <u>shnohr</u>·kehl tah·kih·mih
– a surfboard	– **Surf tahtası** surrf <u>tah</u>·htah·<u>sih</u>
– a towel	– **Havlu** hahv·<u>loo</u>

– an umbrella	– **Şemsiye** <u>shehm</u>·see·ih
– water skis	– **Su kayağı** soo kah·<u>yah</u>·**ih**
– windsurfer	– **Rüzgar sörfçüsü** ryuz·<u>gahr</u> surrf·chyu·syu

Winter Sports

A lift pass for *a day/five days*, please.	***Bir/Beş** günlük teleferik pasosu lütfen.* beer/behsh gyun·lyuk teh·leh·<u>feh</u>·reek pah·soh·soo <u>lyut</u>·fehn
I want to rent [hire]...	**...kiralamak istiyorum.** ...kee·rah·lah·mahk ees·<u>tee</u>·yoh·room
– boots	– **Kayak çizmesi** kah·<u>yahk</u> <u>cheez</u>·meh·see
– a helmet	– **Kask** kahsk
– poles	– **Kayak sopası** kah·<u>yahk</u> soh·pah·sih
– skis	– **Kayak** kah·<u>yahk</u>
– a snowboard	– **Kar kayağı** <u>kahr</u> kah·yah·**ih**
– snowshoes	– **Kar ayakkabısı** <u>kahr</u> ah·yahk·kah·bih·sih
These are too *big/small*.	**Bunlar çok *büyük/küçük*.** boon·<u>lahr</u> chohk byu·<u>yyuk</u>/kyu·<u>chyuk</u>
Are there lessons?	**Ders var mı?** dehrs <u>vahr</u> mih
I'm a beginner.	**Yeni başlıyorum.** yeh·<u>nee</u> bahsh·<u>lih</u>·yoh·room
I'm experienced.	**Deneyimliyim.** deh·neh·yeem·<u>lee</u>·yeem
A trail [piste] map, please.	**Pist haritası lütfen.** peest hah·<u>ree</u>·tah·sih <u>lyut</u>·fehn

i Though most people associate Turkey with a hot climate, Turkey is actually quite mountainous and there is very good skiing to be enjoyed throughout the country. The following is a list of the major ski resorts and their locations: Ankara – Elmadag, outside of Ankara; Antalya – Saklikent, northwest of Antalya; Bolu-Kartalkaya, off the Istanbul - Ankara highway; Bursa – Uludag, just south of Bursa; Erzurum-Palandoken, near Erzurum; Ilgaz Dagi, between Kastamonu and Cankiri; Kars – Sarikamis, close to Kars; Kayseri – Erciyes, near Kayseri and Zigana – Gumushane, just outside of Gumushane.

You May See...

ÇEKİCİ TELEFERİK	drag lift
TELEFERİK	cable car
KOLTUKLU TELEFERİK	chair lift
ACEMİ	novice
ORTA SEVİYEDE	intermediate
UZMAN	expert
PİST KAPALI	trail [piste] closed

In the Countryside

I'd like a map of...	**...haritası istiyorum.** ...hah·<u>ree</u>·tah·sih ees·<u>tee</u>·yoh·room
– this region	– **Bu bölge** boo burl·<u>geh</u>
– walking routes	– **Yürüyüş yolları** yyu·ryu·<u>yyush</u> yohl·lah·rih
– bike routes	– **Bisiklet yolları** bee·see·<u>kleht</u> yohl·lah·rih
– the trails	– **Dar yollar** <u>dahr</u> yohl·lahr
Is it easy?	**Kolay mı?** koh·<u>lie</u> mih

Is it difficult?	**Zor mu?** <u>zohr</u> moo
Is it far?	**Uzak mı?** oo·<u>zahk</u> mih
Is it steep?	**Dik mi?** <u>deek</u> mee
How far is it to...?	**...ne kadar uzakta?** ...<u>neh</u> kah·dahr oo·<u>zahk</u>·tah
Can you show me on the map?	**Bana haritada gösterebilir misiniz?** bah·<u>nah</u> hah·<u>ree</u>·tah·dah gurs·teh·reh·bee·<u>leer</u> mee·see·neez
I'm lost.	**Kayboldum.** <u>kie</u>·bohl·doom
Where's...?	**...nerede?** ...<u>neh</u>·reh·deh
– the bridge	– **Köprü** kurp·<u>ryu</u>
– the cave	– **Mağara** mah·<u>ah</u>·rah
– the cliff	– **Uçurum** oo·choo·<u>room</u>
– the desert	– **Çöl** <u>churl</u>
– the farm	– **Çiftlik** cheeft·<u>leek</u>
– the field	– **Tarla** tahr·<u>lah</u>
– the forest	– **Orman** ohr·<u>mahn</u>
– the hill	– **Tepe** teh·<u>peh</u>
– the lake	– **Göl** gurl
– the mountain	– **Dağ** d<u>ah</u>
– the nature preserve	– **Milli park** meel·<u>lee</u> pahrk
– the overlook	– **Hakim tepe** hah·<u>keem</u> teh·<u>peh</u>
– the park	– **Park** pahrk
– the path	– **Patika** pah·<u>tee</u>·kah
– the peak	– **Tepe** teh·<u>peh</u>
– the picnic area	– **Piknik alanı** peek·<u>neek</u> ah·lah·nih

Where's...?	...nerede? ...neh·reh·deh
– the pond	– **Gölcük** gurl·jyuk
– the river	– **Irmak** ihr·mahk
– the sea	– **Deniz** deh·neez
– the thermal springs	– **Termal kaynaklar** tehr·mahl kie·nahk·lahr
– the stream	– **Dere** deh·reh
– the valley	– **Vadi** vah·dee
– the vineyard/ winery	– **Bağ/Şaraphane** bah/shah·rahp·hah·neh
– the waterfall	– **Şelale** sheh·lah·leh

Culture and Nightlife

Essential

What is there to do in the evenings?	**Geceleri ne yapılır?** geh·jeh·leh·ree neh yah·pih·lihr
Do you have a program of events?	**Bir rehberiniz var mı?** beer reh·beh·ree·neez vahr mih
What's playing at the movies [cinema] tonight?	**Bu gece hangi filmler oynuyor?** boo geh·jeh hahn·gee feelm·lehr oy·noo·yohr
Where's...?	...nerede? ...neh·reh·deh
– the downtown area	– **Kent merkezi** kehnt mehr·keh·zee
– the bar	– **Bar** bahr
– the dance club	– **Diskotek** dees·koh·tehk
Is there a cover charge?	**Giriş ücretli mi?** gee·reesh yuj·reht·lee mee

i

Culturally, Turkey has a lot to offer. There are numerous archeological sites spread throughout the country, which represent many different periods in history. The ruins at **Efes** (Ephesus), for example, are certainly worth a trip. Though the area was inhabited over 6000 years ago, during the Neolithic period, and traces have been excavated from various periods since then, the well-conserved ruins you can visit today are mainly from Roman times, that is, they are more than 2000 years old.

Moreover, there is no shortage of theaters, operas, concert halls and museums, particularly in the larger cities. And many cities in Turkey are host to excellent music, film and dance festivals throughout the year. Visit the local **Turizm Danışma Bürosu** (tourist information offices) to find out what's going on while you are in town.

Entertainment

Can you recommend...?	**...önerebilir misiniz?** ...ur·neh·reh·bee·<u>leer</u> mee·see·neez
– a concert	– **Konser** kohn·<u>sehr</u>
– a movie	– **Film** feelm
– an opera	– **Opera** oh·<u>peh</u>·rah
– a play	– **Tiyatro oyunu** tee·<u>yaht</u>·roh oh·<u>yoo</u>·noo
When does it *start/end*?	**Ne zaman *başlıyor/bitiyor?*** neh zah·<u>mahn</u> bahsh·<u>lih</u>·yohr/bee·<u>tee</u>·yohr
What's the dress code?	**Giyim tarzı ne?** gee·<u>yeem</u> tahr·<u>zih</u> neh
I like...	**...severim.** ...seh·<u>veh</u>·reem
– classical music	– **Klasik müzik** klah·<u>seek</u> myu·<u>zeek</u>
– folk music	– **Halk müziği** <u>hahlk</u> myu·zee·<u>yee</u>
– jazz	– **Caz** jahz

139

I like...	...severim. ...seh·<u>veh</u>·reem
– pop music	– **Pop** pohp
– rap	– **Rep** rehp

▶ For ticketing, see page 18.

You May Hear...

Cep telefonlarınızı kapatınız lütfen. <u>jehp</u> teh·leh·fohn·lah·rih·nih·<u>zih</u> kah·<u>pah</u>·tih·nihz <u>lyut</u>·fehn	Turn off your cell [mobile] phones, please.

Nightlife

What is there to do in the evenings?	**Geceleri ne yapılır?** geh·jeh·leh·<u>ree</u> neh <u>yah</u>·pih·lihr
Can you recommend...?	**...önerebilir misiniz?** ...ur·neh·reh·bee·<u>leer</u> mee·see·neez
– a bar	– **Bar** bahr
– a casino	– **Kumarhane** koo·mahr·hah·<u>neh</u>
– a dance club	– **Diskotek** <u>dees</u>·koh·tehk
– a gay club	– **Eşcinsel klübü** <u>ehsh</u>·jeen·sehl klyu·<u>byu</u>
– a nightclub	– **Gece klübü** geh·<u>jeh</u> klyu·<u>byu</u>
Is there live music?	**Orada canlı müzik var mı?** <u>oh</u>·rah·dah <u>jahn</u>·lih myu·<u>zeek</u> vahr mih
How do I get there?	**Oraya nasıl gidebilirim?** <u>oh</u>·rah·yah <u>nah</u>·sihl gee·deh·bee·lee·reem
Is there a cover charge?	**Masa ücreti var mı?** mah·<u>sah</u> yuj·reh·<u>tee</u> <u>vahr</u> mih
Let's go dancing.	**Hadi dans etmeye gidelim.** hah·<u>dee</u> dans eht·meh·yeh gee·deh·<u>leem</u>

▼ Special Needs

Business Travel

Essential

I'm here on business.	**İş için burdayım.** <u>eesh</u> ee·cheen boor·<u>dah</u>·yihm
Here's my business card.	**Buyrun kartvizitim.** <u>booy</u>·roon kahrt·vee·zee·<u>teem</u>
Can I have your card?	**Kartınızı alabilirmiyim?** kahr·tih·nih·<u>zih</u> ah·lah·bee·<u>leer</u> mee·yeem
I have a meeting with...	**...ile bir randevum var.** ...ee·<u>leh</u> beer rahn·deh·<u>voom</u> vahr
Where's...?	**...nerede?** ...<u>neh</u>·reh·deh
– the business center	– **İş merkezi** <u>eesh</u> mehr·keh·zee
– the convention hall	– **Kongre salonu** kohng·<u>reh</u> sah·loh·<u>noo</u>
– the meeting room	– **Toplantı odası** tohp·<u>lahn</u>·tih oh·<u>dah</u>·sih

Business Communication

I'm here to attend...	**...katılmak için burdayım.** ...kah·<u>tihl</u>·mahk ee·cheen boor·<u>dah</u>·yihm
– a seminar	– **Seminere** seh·<u>mee</u>·nehr
– a conference	– **Konferansa** kohn·feh·<u>rahn</u>·sah
– a meeting	– **Toplantıya** tohp·lahn·tih·<u>yah</u>
My name is...	**İsmim...** ees·<u>meem</u>...
May I introduce my colleague...?	**...meslektaşımı tanıtabilir miyim?** ...mehs·lehk·<u>tah</u>·shih·mih tah·<u>nih</u>·tah·bee·<u>leer</u> mee·yeem

I have *a meeting/ an appointment* with...	**...ile bir *toplantım/randevum* var.**	...ee·<u>leh</u> beer *tohp·lahn·<u>tihm</u>/rahn·deh·<u>voom</u>* vahr
I'm sorry I'm late.	**Üzgünüm, geciktim.**	yuz·<u>gyu</u>·nyum geh·jeek·<u>teem</u>
I need an interpreter.	**Tercüman istiyorum.**	tehr·jyu·<u>mahn</u> ees·<u>tee</u>·yoh·room
You can reach me at the...Hotel.	**...otelden bana ulaşabilirsin.**	...oh·tehl·<u>dehn</u> bah·<u>nah</u> oo·lah·shah·bee·<u>leer</u>·seen
I'm here until...	**...kadar burdayım.**	...kah·<u>dahr</u> boor·<u>dah</u>·yihm
I need to...	**...gerek.**	...yahp·<u>mahm</u> geh·rehk
– make a call	**– Telefon görüşmesi yapmam**	teh·leh·<u>fohn</u> gur·ryush·meh·<u>see</u>
– make a photocopy	**– Bir fotokopi yapmam**	beer foh·toh·koh·<u>pee</u>

143

I need to...	**...gerek.** ...yahp·<u>mahm</u> geh·rehk
– send an e-mail	– **E-posta göndermem** eh·pohs·<u>tah</u> gurn·dehr·<u>mehm</u>
– send a fax	– **Faks çekmem** <u>fahks</u> chehk·<u>mehm</u>
– send a package	– **Paket göndermem** pah·<u>keht</u> gurn·dehr·<u>mehm</u>
It was a pleasure to meet you.	**Sizinle tanışmaktan memnun oldum.** see·<u>zeen</u>·leh tah·nihsh·mahk·<u>tahn</u> mehm·<u>noon</u> ohl·doom

▶ For internet and communications, see page 47.

i When people meet in a professional setting, generally they shake hands and say **merhaba** (hello). Drinking small cups of tea throughout the day is a common practice in places of business, and visitors are likely to be offered tea as well. Note that some traditional people avoid shaking hands with people they are meeting for the first time. If so, this will be evident in their behavior (not offering a hand, staying several feet away). In such circumstances, an exchange of verbal greetings, eye contact and smiles should suffice.

You May Hear...

Randevunuz mu var? rahn·deh·voo·<u>nooz</u> moo vahr	Do you have an appointment?
Kiminle? kee·<u>meen</u>·leh	With whom?
O toplantıda. oh tohp·lahn·tih·<u>dah</u>	*He/She* is in a meeting.
Bir dakika lütfen. beer dah·<u>kee</u>·kah <u>lyut</u>·fehn	One moment, please.
Oturun. oh·<u>too</u>·roon	Have a seat.

İçecek birşeyler istermisiniz? ee·cheh·<u>jehk</u> beer shay·<u>lehr</u> ees·<u>tehr</u>·mee·see·neez | Would you like something to drink?

Geldiğiniz için teşekkürler. gehl·dee·ee·<u>neez</u> ee·cheen teh·shehk·kyur·<u>lehr</u> | Thank you for coming.

Travel with Children

Essential

Is there a discount for children? | **Çocuklar için indirim var mı?** choh·jook·<u>lahr</u> ee·<u>cheen</u> een·dee·<u>reem</u> vahr mih

Can you recommend a babysitter? | **Bir çocuk bakıcısı önerebilir misiniz?** beer choh·<u>jook</u> bah·kih·jih·<u>sih</u> ur·neh·reh·bee·<u>leer</u> mee·see·neez

145

Could we have a *child's seat/highchair*?	***Çocuk sandalyesi/Yüksek sandalye alabilir miyiz?*** *choh·jook sahn·dahl·yeh·see/yyuk·sehk sahn·dahl·yeh* ah·lah·bee·leer mee·yeez
Where can I change the baby?	**Bebeğin altını nerede değiştirebilirim?** beh·beh·yeen ahl·tih·nih neh·reh·deh deh·yeesh·tee·reh·bee·lee·reem

Fun with Kids

Can you recommend something for the kids?	**Çocuklar için birşeyler önerir misiniz?** choh·jook·lahr ee·cheen beer shay·lehr ur·neh·reer mee·see·neez
Where's...?	**...nerede?** ...neh·reh·deh
– the amusement park	**– Oyun parkı** oh·yoon pahr·kih
– the arcade	**– Oyun salonu** oh·yoon sah·loh·noo
– the kiddie [paddling] pool	**– Çocuk havuzu** choh·jook hah·voo·zoo
– the park	**– Park** pahrk
– the playground	**– Çocuk parkı** choh·jook pahr·kih
– the zoo	**– Hayvanat bahçesi** hie·vah·naht bah·cheh·see
Are kids allowed?	**Çocuklara serbest mi?** choh·jook·lah·rah sehr·behst mee
Is it safe for kids?	**Çocuklar için güvenli mi?** choh·jook·lahr ee·cheen gyu·vehn·lee mee
Is it suitable for...year olds?	**...yaş için uygun mu?** ...yash ee·cheen ooy·goon moo

▶ For numbers, see page 169.

You May Hear...

Ne kadar sevimli! neh kah·dahr seh·veem·<u>lee</u> — How cute!

İsmi ne? ees·<u>mee</u> neh — What's *his/her* name?

Kaç yaşında? <u>kach</u> yah·shihn·dah — How old is *he/she*?

Basic Needs for Kids

Do you have...?	**...var mı?** ...<u>vahr</u> mih
– a baby bottle	– **Biberon** bee·beh·<u>rohn</u>
– baby wipes	– **Bebek mendili** beh·<u>behk</u> mehn·dee·lee
– a car seat	– **Araba koltuğu** ah·rah·<u>bah</u> kohl·too·<u>oo</u>
– a children's menu/portion	– **Çocuk *menüsü/porsiyonu*** choh·<u>jook</u> meh·nyu·<u>syu</u>/pohr·see·yoh·<u>noo</u>
– a child's seat	– **Çocuk sandalyesi** choh·<u>jook</u> sahn·dahl·yeh·<u>see</u>
– a cot	– **Çocuk Beşik** choh·<u>jook</u> beh·sheek
– a crib	– **Çocuk yatağı** choh·<u>jook</u> yah·<u>tah</u>·ih
– diapers [nappies]	– **Bebek bezi** beh·<u>bek</u> beh·zee
– formula	– **Formül** fohr·<u>myul</u>
– a highchair	– **Çocuk Yüksek sandalye** choh·<u>jook</u> yyuk·<u>sehk</u> sahn·dahl·<u>yeh</u>
– a pacifier [soother]	– **Yatıştırıcı** yah·tihsh·tih·rih·<u>jih</u>
– a playpen	– **Portatif çocuk parkı** pohr·tah·<u>teef</u> choh·<u>jook</u> pahr·kih
– a stroller [push chair]	– **Puset** poo·<u>seht</u>
Can I breastfeed the baby here?	**Bebeği burda emzirebilir miyim?** beh·beh·<u>yee</u> boor·dah ehm·zee·reh·bee·<u>leer</u> mee·yeem

| Where can I change the baby? | **Bebeğin altını nerede değiştirebilirim?** beh·beh·<u>yeen</u> ahl·tih·<u>nih</u> <u>neh</u>·reh·deh deh·yeesh·tee·reh·bee·<u>lee</u>·reem |

▶ For dining with kids, see page 63.

Babysitting

Can you recommend a babysitter?	**Bir çocuk bakıcısı önerebilir misiniz?** beer choh·<u>jook</u> bah·kih·jih·<u>sih</u> ur·neh·reh·bee·<u>leer</u> mee·see·neez
What's the charge?	**Ücreti nedir?** yuj·reh·<u>tee</u> neh·deer
We'll be back by...	**...kadar geri döneriz.** ...kah·dahr geh·<u>ree</u> dur·neh·reez

▶ For time, see page 171.

| I can be reached at... | **Bana...ulaşabilirsiniz.** bah·<u>nah</u>... oo·lah·shah·bee·<u>leer</u>·see·neez |

▶ For numbers, see page 169.

Health and Emergency

Can you recommend a pediatrician?	**Bir çocuk doktoru önerir misiniz?** beer choh·<u>jook</u> dohk·toh·<u>roo</u> ur·neh·<u>reer</u> mee·see·neez
My child is allergic to...	**Çocuğumun...alerjisi var.** choh·joo·oo·<u>moon</u>...ah·lehr·jee·see vahr
My child is missing.	**Çocuğum kayıp.** choh·joo·**oom** kah·yihp
Have you seen a *boy/girl*?	**Bir *oğlan/kız* gördünüz mü?** beer oo·<u>lahn</u>/ kihz gurr·dyu·<u>nyuz</u> myu

▶ For food items, see page 84.

▶ For health, see page 154.

▶ For police, see page 152.

For the Disabled

Essential

Is there...?	**...var mı?** ...vahr mih
– access for the disabled	– **Engelli girişi** ehn·gehl·<u>lee</u> gee·ree·<u>shee</u>
– a wheelchair ramp	– **Tekerlekli sandalye rampası** teh·kehr·lehk·<u>lee</u> sahn·<u>dahl</u>·yeh rahm·pah·sih
– a handicapped- [disabled-] accessible restroom [toilet]	– **Özürlü tuvaleti** ur·zyur·<u>lyu</u> too·<u>vah</u>·leh·tee
I need...	**...ihtiyacım var.** ...eeh·tee·yah·<u>jihm</u> vahr
– assistance	– **Yardımcıya** yahr·dihm·jih·<u>yah</u>
– an elevator [lift]	– **Asansöre** ah·sahn·sur·<u>reh</u>
– a ground-floor room	– **Zemin-kat odasına** zeh·<u>meen</u>·kaht oh·dah·sih·<u>nah</u>

149

Getting Help

I'm disabled. **Ben özürlüyüm.** behn ur·zyur·*lyu*·yyum

I'm deaf. **Ben sağırım.** behn s**ah**·*ih*·rihm

I'm *visually/ hearing* impaired. **Görme/Duyma engelliyim.** gurr·*meh*/ dooy·*mah* ehn·gel·*lee*·yeem

I'm unable to walk far. **Uzağa yürüyemem.** oo·zah·**ah** yyu·ryu·*yeh*·mehm

I'm unable to use the stairs. **Merdivenleri kullanamam.** mehr·dee·vehn·leh·*ree* kool·lah·*nah*·mahm

Can I bring my wheelchair? **Tekerlekli sandalyemi getirebilir miyim?** teh·kehr·lehk·*lee* sahn·*dahl*·yeh·mee geh·tee·reh·bee·*leer* mee·yeem

Are guide dogs permitted? **Rehber köpeklere izin var mı?** reh·*behr* kur·pehk·leh·*reh* ee·zeen *vahr* mih

Can you help me? **Bana yardım edebilir misiniz?** bah·*nah* yahr·*dihm* eh·deh·bee·*leer* mee·see·neez

Please *open/hold* the door. **Lütfen kapıyı *açın/tutun.*** *lyut*·fehn kah·*pih*·yih *ah*·chihn/*too*·toon

▼ Resources

Emergencies

Essential

Help!	**İmdat!** eem·<u>daht</u>
Go away!	**Çekil git!** cheh·<u>keel</u> geet
Stop thief!	**Durdurun, hırsız!** door·<u>doo</u>·roon hihr·<u>sihz</u>
Get a doctor!	**Bir doktor bulun!** beer dohk·<u>tohr</u> boo·loon
Fire!	**Yangın!** yahn·<u>gihn</u>
I'm lost.	**Kayboldum.** kie·bohl·doom
Can you help me?	**Bana yardım edebilir misiniz?** bah·nah yahr·<u>dihm</u> eh·deh·bee·<u>leer</u> mee·see·neez

Police

Essential

Call the police!	**Polis çağırın!** poh·<u>lees</u> <u>chah</u>·ih·rihn
Where's the police station?	**Karakol nerede?** kah·rah·<u>kohl</u> <u>neh</u>·reh·deh
There has been an *accident/attack*.	**Bir *kaza/saldırı* oldu.** beer kah·<u>zah</u>/ sahl·<u>dih</u>·rih ohl·doo
My child is missing.	**Çocuğum kayıp.** choh·joo·<u>oom</u> kah·<u>yihp</u>
I need...	**...ihtiyacım var.** ...eeh·tee·yah·<u>jihm</u> vahr
– an interpreter	**– Tercümana** tehr·jyu·mah·<u>nah</u>
– to contact my lawyer	**– Avukatımla görüşmeye** ah·voo·kah·<u>tihm</u>·lah gur·ryush·meh·<u>yeh</u>
– to make a phone call	**– Telefon görüşmesi yapmaya** teh·leh·<u>fohn</u> gur·ryush·meh·<u>see</u> yahp·mah·<u>yah</u>
I'm innocent.	**Masumum.** mah·<u>soo</u>·moom

You May Hear...

Bu formu doldurun lütfen. boo <u>fohr</u>·moo dohl·<u>doo</u>·roon <u>lyut</u>·fehn

Please fill out this form.

Kimliğiniz lütfen. keem·lee·yee·<u>neez</u> <u>lyut</u>·fehn

Your identification, please.

Ne zaman/Nerede oldu? <u>neh</u> zah·mahn/ <u>neh</u>·reh·deh ohl·doo

When/Where did it happen?

Nasıl biriydi? <u>nah</u>·sihl bee·<u>reey</u>·dee

What did *he/she* look like?

Lost Property and Theft

I want to report...	**Bir...haber vermek istiyorum.** beer...hah·<u>behr</u> vehr·mehk ees·<u>tee</u>·yoh·room
– a mugging	– **gasp** gahsp
– a rape	– **tecavüz** teh·jah·<u>vyuz</u>
– a theft	– **hırsızlık** hihr·sihz·<u>lihk</u>
I've been *robbed/ mugged*.	**Çarpıldım/Soyuldum.** chah·rpihl·dihm/ soh·yool·<u>doom</u>
I've lost my...	**...kaybettim.** ...<u>kie</u>·beht·teem
My...has been stolen.	**...çalındı.** ...chah·lihn·<u>dih</u>
– backpack	– **Sırt çantam** sihrt chahn·<u>tahm</u>
– bicycle	– **Bisikletim** bee·seek·leh·<u>teem</u>
– camera	– **Fotoğraf makinem** foh·toh·<u>rahf</u> mah·kee·<u>nehm</u>
– (rental) car	– **(Kiralık) Arabam** (kee·rah·<u>lihk</u>) ah·rah·<u>bahm</u>
– computer	– **Bilgisayarım** beel·gee·sah·yah·<u>rihm</u>

My...has been stolen.	...çalındı. ...chah·lihn·<u>dih</u>
– credit card	– **Kredi kartlarım** kreh·<u>dee</u> kahrt·lah·<u>rihm</u>
– jewelry	– **Mücevheratım** myu·jehv·heh·rah·<u>tihm</u>
– money	– **Param** pah·<u>rahm</u>
– passport	– **Pasaportum** pah·sah·pohr·<u>toom</u>
– purse [handbag]	– **Cüzdanım** jyuz·dah·<u>nihm</u>
– traveler's checks [cheques]	– **Seyahat çeklerim** seh·yah·<u>haht</u> chehk·leh·<u>reem</u>
– wallet	– **Cüzdanım** jyuz·<u>dah</u>·nihm
I need a police report.	**Polis raporuna ihtiyacım var.** poh·<u>lees</u> rah·poh·rooh·<u>nah</u> eeh·tee·yah·<u>jihm</u> vahr

Health

Essential

I'm sick [ill].	**Hastayım.** hahs·<u>tah</u>·yihm
I need an English-speaking doctor.	**İngilizce konuşan bir doktora ihtiyacım var.** een·gee·<u>leez</u>·jeh koh·noo·<u>shahn</u> beer dohk·toh·<u>rah</u> eeh·tee·yah·<u>jihm</u> vahr
It hurts here.	**Burası acıyor.** <u>boo</u>·rah·sih ah·<u>jih</u>·yohr
I have a stomachache.	**Mide ağrım var.** mee·<u>deh</u> **ah**·<u>rihm</u> vahr

Finding a Doctor

Can you recommend a *doctor/dentist*?	**Bir *doktor/dişçi* önerir misiniz?** beer dohk·<u>tohr</u>/<u>deesh</u>·chee ur·neh·<u>reer</u> mee·see·neez

Could the doctor come to see me here?	**Doktor beni gelip burada görebilir mi?** dohk·<u>tohr</u> beh·<u>nee</u> geh·<u>leep</u> boo·rah·dah gur·reh·bee·<u>leer</u> mee
I need an English-speaking doctor.	**İngilizce konuşan bir doktora ihtiyacım var.** een·gee·<u>leez</u>·jeh koh·noo·<u>shahn</u> beer dohk·toh·<u>rah</u> eeh·tee·yah·<u>jihm</u> vahr
What are the office hours?	**Çalışma saatleri nedir?** chah·lihsh·<u>mah</u> sah·aht·leh·<u>ree</u> neh·deer
Can I make an appointment...?	**...için randevu alabilir miyim?** ...ee·<u>cheen</u> rahn·deh·<u>voo</u> ah·lah·bee·<u>leer</u> mee·yeem
– for today	**– Bugün** boo·gyun
– for tomorrow	**– Yarın** yah·<u>rihn</u>
– as soon as possible	**– En yakın zaman** ehn yah·<u>kihn</u> zah·<u>mahn</u>
It's urgent.	**Acil.** ah·<u>jeel</u>

▶ For time, see page 171.

Symptoms

I'm bleeding.	**Kanamam var.** kah·nah·<u>mahm</u> vahr
I'm constipated.	**Kabızım.** kah·<u>bih</u>·zihm
I'm dizzy.	**Başım dönüyor.** bah·<u>shihm</u> dur·<u>nyu</u>·yohr
I'm *nauseous/ vomiting*.	**Bulantım var./Kusuyorum.** boo·lahn·<u>tihm</u> vahr/koo·<u>soo</u>·yoh·room
It hurts here.	**Burası acıyor.** boo·rah·<u>sih</u> ah·<u>jih</u>·yohr
I have...	**...var.** ...vahr
– an allergic reaction	**– Alerjik reaksiyonum** ah·lehr·<u>jeek</u> reh·ahk·see·yoh·<u>noom</u>
– chest pain	**– Göğüs ağrım** gur·<u>yus</u> **ah**·rihm

155

I have...	...var. ...vahr
– an earache	– **Kulak ağrım** koo·<u>lahk</u> **ah**·<u>rihm</u>
– a fever	– **Ateşim** ah·teh·<u>sheem</u>
– pain	– **Ağrım ah**·<u>rihm</u>
– a rash	– **Kaşıntım** kah·shihn·<u>tihm</u>
– a sprain	– **Burkulmam** boor·kool·<u>mahm</u>
– some swelling	– **Şişliğim** sheesh·<u>lee</u>·eem
– a stomachache	– **Mide ağrım** mee·<u>deh</u> **ah**·<u>rihm</u>
– sunstroke	– **Güneş çarpmam** gyu·<u>nehsh</u> chahrp·<u>mahm</u>
I've been sick [ill] for...days.	...**gündür hastayım.** ...<u>gyun</u>·dyur hahs·<u>tah</u>·yihm

▶ For numbers, see page 169.

Health Conditions

I'm...	**Ben...** ben...
– anemic	– **anemi hastasıyım** ah·neh·<u>mee</u> hahs·tah·<u>sih</u>·yihm
– diabetic	– **şeker hastasıyım** sheh·<u>kehr</u> hahs·tah·<u>sih</u>·yihm
– asthmatic	– **astım** ahs·<u>tihm</u>
I'm allergic to *antibiotics/ penicillin.*	***Antibiyotiğe/Penisiline alerjim var.*** *ahn·tee·bee·yoh·tee·<u>yeh</u>/peh·nee·see·lee·<u>neh</u> ah·lehr·<u>jeem</u> vahr*

▶ For food items, see page 84.

I have arthritis.	**Artiritim.** ahr·tee·ree·<u>teem</u>
I have (high/low) blood pressure.	**(*Yüksek/ Düşük*) Tansiyonum var.** (*yyuk·<u>sehk</u>/dyu·<u>shyuk</u>*) tahn·see·yoh·<u>noom</u> vahr

| I have a heart condition. | **Kalbimden rahatsızım.** kahl·beem·<u>dehn</u> rah·hat·<u>sih</u>·zihm |
| I'm on... | **...dayım.** ...<u>dah</u>·yihm |

You May Hear...

Sorununuz ne? soh·roo·noo·<u>nooz</u> <u>neh</u>	What's wrong?
Neresi acıyor? <u>neh</u>·reh·see ah·<u>jih</u>·yohr	Where does it hurt?
Burası acıyor mu? <u>boo</u>·rah·sih ah·<u>jih</u>·yohr moo	Does it hurt here?
Başka ilaç alıyor musunuz? bahsh·<u>kah</u> ee·<u>lahch</u> ah·<u>lih</u>·yohr moo·soo·nooz	Are you taking any other medication?
Herhangi bir şeye alerjiniz var mı? hehr·<u>hahn</u>·gee beer sheh·yeh ah·lehr·jee·<u>neez</u> <u>vahr</u> mih	Are you allergic to anything?
Ağzınızı açın. ah·zih·nih·<u>zih</u> <u>ah</u>·chihn	Open your mouth.
Derin nefes alın. deh·<u>reen</u> neh·<u>fes</u> ah·lihn	Breathe deeply.
Hastaneye gitmenizi istiyorum. hahs·tah·neh·<u>yeh</u> geet·meh·nee·<u>zee</u> ees·<u>tee</u>·yoh·room	I want you to go to the hospital.

Hospital

Please notify my family.	**Lütfen aileme bildirin.** <u>lyut</u>·fehn ah·ee·leh·<u>meh</u> beel·<u>dee</u>·reen
I'm in pain.	**Acı içindeyim.** ah·<u>jih</u> ee·cheen·<u>deh</u>·yeem
I need a *doctor/ nurse*.	***Doktora/Hemşireye* ihtiyacım var.** dohk·toh·<u>rah</u>/hehm·shee·reh·<u>yeh</u> eeh·tee·yah·<u>jihm</u> vahr
When are visiting hours?	**Ziyaret saatleri ne zaman?** zee·yah·<u>reht</u> sah·aht·leh·<u>ree</u> <u>neh</u> zah·mahn

| I'm visiting... | **...ziyaret edeceğim.** ...zee·yah·reht eh·deh·jeh·yeem |

Dentist

I've *broken a tooth/ lost a filling*.	**Dişim kırıldı./Dolgumu düşürdüm.** dee·sheem kih·rihl·dih/dohl·goo·moo dyu·shyur·dyum
I have a toothache.	**Dişim ağrıyor.** dee·sheem **ah**·rih·yohr
Can you fix this denture?	**Bu protezi onarabilir misiniz?** boo proh·teh·zee oh·nah·rah·bee·leer mee·see·neez

Gynecologist

I have menstrual cramps.	**Aybaşı ağrım.** ie·bah·shih **ah**·rihm
I have a vaginal infection.	**Vajina iltihaplanması var.** vah·jee·nah eel·tee·hahp·lahn·mah·sih vahr
I missed my period.	**Günüm gecikti.** gyu·nyum geh·jeek·tee
I'm on the Pill.	**Doğum kontrol hapı kullanıyorum.** doh·oom kohnt·rohl hah·pih kool·lah·nih·yoh·room
I'm pregnant.	**Hamileyim.** hah·mee·leh·yeem
I'm not pregnant.	**Hamile değilim.** hah·mee·leh deh·yee·leem
I haven't had my period for...months.	**...aydan beri aybaşım olmuyor.** ...ie·dahn beh·ree ie·bah·shihm ohl·moo·yohr

▶ For numbers, see page 169.

Optician

| I've lost... | **...kaybettim.** ...kie·beht·teem |
| – a contact lens | – **Bir kontak lensimi** beer kohn·tahk lehn·see·mee |

– my glasses	**– Gözlüğümü** gurz·lyu·yu·<u>myu</u>
– a lens	**– Camımı** jah·mih·<u>mih</u>

Payment and Insurance

How much?	**Ne kadar?** <u>neh</u> kah·dahr
Can I pay by credit card?	**Bu kredi kartı ile ödeme yapabilir miyim?** boo <u>kreh</u>·dee kahr·<u>tih</u> ee·<u>leh</u> ur·deh·meh yah·pah·bee·<u>leer</u> mee·yeem
I have insurance.	**Sigortam var.** see·gohr·<u>tahm</u> vahr
Can I have a receipt for my insurance?	**Sigorta için fiş alabilir miyim?** see·gohr·<u>tah</u> ee·cheen <u>feesh</u> ah·lah·bee·<u>leer</u> mee·yeem

Pharmacy [Chemist]

Essential

Where's the nearest pharmacy [chemist]?	**En yakın eczane nerede?** <u>ehn</u> yah·<u>kihn</u> ehj·zah·<u>neh</u> <u>neh</u>·reh·deh
What time does the pharmacy *open/ close* [chemist]?	**Eczane ne zaman *açılıyor/kapanıyor*?** ehj·zah·<u>neh</u> <u>neh</u> zah·mahn *ah·chih·<u>lih</u>·yohr/ kah·pah·<u>nih</u>·yohr*
What would you recommend for...?	**...için ne önerirdiniz?** ...ee·cheen <u>neh</u> ur·neh·<u>reer</u>·dee·neez
How much should I take?	**Ne kadar almalıyım?** <u>neh</u> kah·dahr ahl·mah·<u>lih</u>·yihm
Can you fill [make up] this prescription for me?	**Bana bu reçeteyi hazırlar mısınız?** bah·nah boo reh·<u>cheh</u>·teh·yee hah·zihr·<u>lahr</u> mih·sih·nihz
I'm allergic to...	**...alerjim var.** ...ah·lehr·<u>jeem</u> vahr

_i_
In Turkey, the **eczane** (pharmacy) fills medical prescriptions and sells non-prescription drugs as well as cosmetics. Regular hours are generally Monday to Saturday from 9 a.m. to 7 p.m. At other times, pharmacies work on a rotating schedule. Check the store window to find the closest **nöbetçi eczane** (all-night pharmacy).

Dosage Instructions

How much should I take?	**Ne kadar almalıyım?** <u>neh</u> kah·dahr ahl·mah·<u>lih</u>·yihm
How often?	**Günde kaç defa almalıyım?** gyun·<u>deh</u> <u>kahch</u> deh·fah ahl·mah·<u>lih</u>·yihm
Is it suitable for children?	**Çocuklar için uygun mu?** choh·jook·<u>lahr</u> ee·cheen ooy·<u>goon</u> moo
I'm taking...	**...alıyorum.** ...ah·<u>lih</u>·yoh·room

| Are there side effects? | **Yan etkisi var mı?** <u>yahn</u> eht·kee·<u>see</u> <u>vahr</u> mih |

You May See...

GÜNDE *BİR*/*ÜÇ* KERE	*once*/*three* times a day
TABLET	tablet
DAMLA	drop
ÇAY KAŞIĞI	teaspoon
YEMEKDEN ÖNCE	before meals
YEMEKDEN SONRA	after meals
YEMEKLERLE BİRLİKTE	with meals
AÇ KARNINA	on an empty stomach
BÜTÜN YUTUN	swallow whole
UYKUYA YOL AÇABILIR	may cause drowsiness
İÇİLMEZ	for external use only

Health Problems

I'd like some medicine for...	**...için bir ilaç istiyorum.** ...ee·cheen beer ee·<u>lahch</u> ees·<u>tee</u>·yoh·room
– a cold	– **Soğuk algınlığı** soh·<u>ook</u> ahl·gihn·lih·<u>ih</u>
– a cough	– **Öksürük** urk·syu·<u>ryuk</u>
– diarrhea	– **İshal** ees·<u>hahl</u>
– insect bites	– **Böcek sokması** bur·<u>jehk</u> sohk·mah·<u>sih</u>

I'd like some medicine for...	**...için bir ilaç istiyorum.** ...ee·cheen beer ee·<u>lahch</u> ees·<u>tee</u>·yoh·room
– motion [travel] sickness	– **Yol tutması** yohl toot·mah·<u>sih</u>
– a sore throat	– **Boğaz ağrısı** boh·<u>ahz</u> **ah**·rih·sih
– sunburn	– **Güneş yanığı** gyu·<u>nehsh</u> yah·nih·ih
– an upset stomach	– **Mide bozukluğu** mee·<u>deh</u> boh·zook·loo·**<u>oo</u>**

Basic Needs

I'd like...	**...istiyorum.** ...ees·<u>tee</u>·yoh·room
– acetaminophen [paracetamol]	– **Parasetamol** pah·rah·<u>seh</u>·tah·<u>mohl</u>
– antiseptic cream	– **Antiseptik krem** ahn·tee·sehp·<u>teek</u> krehm
– aspirin	– **Aspirin** ahs·pee·<u>reen</u>
– bandages [plasters]	– **Bandaj** bahn·<u>dahj</u>
– a comb	– **Tarak** tah·<u>rahk</u>
– condoms	– **Prezervatif** preh·zehr·vah·<u>teef</u>
– contact lens solution	– **Kontakt lens solüsyonu** kohn·<u>tahkt</u> lehns soh·lyus·yoh·<u>noo</u>
– deodorant	– **Deodorant** deh·oh·doh·<u>rahnt</u>
– a hairbrush	– **Saç fırçası** <u>sahch</u> fihr·chah·sih
– hair spray	– **Saç spreyi** <u>sahch</u> spreh·yee
– ibuprofen	– **Ibuprofen** ee·<u>boop</u>·roh·<u>fehn</u>
– insect repellent	– **Böcek kovucu** bur·<u>jek</u> koh·voo·joo
– a nail file	– **Tırnak törpüsü** tihr·<u>nahk</u> turr·pyu·<u>syu</u>

– a (disposable) razor	– **(Tek kullanımlık) Jilet** (<u>tehk</u> kool·lah·nihm·<u>lihk</u>) jee·<u>leht</u>
– razor blades	– **Jilet** jee·<u>leht</u>
– sanitary napkins [pads]	– **Âdet bezi** ah·<u>deht</u> beh·<u>zee</u>
– shampoo/ conditioner	– **Şampuan/Saç kremi** shahm·poo·<u>ahn</u>/ <u>sahch</u> kreh·mee
– soap	– **Sabun** sah·<u>boon</u>
– sunscreen	– **Güneş geçirmez krem** gyu·<u>nehsh</u> geh·cheer·<u>mehz</u> krehm
– tampons	– **Tampon** tahm·<u>pohn</u>
– tissues	– **Kağıt mendil** kah·<u>iht</u> mehn·<u>deel</u>
– toilet paper	– **Tuvalet kağıdı** too·<u>vah</u>·leht kah·<u>ih</u>·dih
– a toothbrush	– **Diş fırçası** <u>deesh</u> fihr·çah·<u>sih</u>
– toothpaste	– **Diş macunu** <u>deesh</u> mah·joo·noo

▶ For baby products, see page 147.

Reference

Grammar

Regular Verbs

Turkish verbs use a stem with suffixes to indicate tense (present, past, future) and person. The stem of the verb can be found by removing **mak** or **mek** from the infinitive of the verb, e.g. the stem of **gezmek** (to travel) is **gez**; the stem of **açmak** (to open) is **aç**. The past tense has the suffix **–d–**, and the future, the suffix **–ecek–**.

form. = formal	inf. = informal	sing. = singular	pl. = plural

Following are the present, past and future conjugations of the verb **gezmek** (to travel).

gezmek (to travel)		Present	Past	Future
I	ben	gezerim	gezdim	gezeceğim
you (sing., inf.)	sen	gezersin	gezdin	gezeceksin
he/she/it	o	gezer	gezdi	gezecek
we	biz	gezeriz	gezdik	gezeceğiz
you (pl./ form.)	siz	gezersiniz	gezdiniz	gezeceksiniz
they	onlar	gezerler	gezdiler	gezecekler

To form the present continuous tense (which can also be used for future), the suffix –iyor– is added to the stem, followed by personal suffixes (see below).

gezmek (to travel)		Present continuous	Past	Future
I	ben	geziyorum	geziyordum	geziyor olacağım
you (sing., inf.)	sen	geziyorsun	geziyordun	geziyor olacaksın
he/she/it	o	geziyor	geziyordu	geziyor olacak
we	biz	geziyoruz	geziyorduk	geziyor olacağız
you (pl./ form.)	siz	geziyorsunuz	geziyordunuz	geziyor olacaksınız
they	onlar	geziyorlar	geziyorlardı	geziyor olacaklar

Irregular Verbs

Turkish is rather remarkable among living languages in having a highly regular verb conjugation system. A minor irregularity is found in about a dozen verbs where the present general takes a vowel-harmony congruent vowel after the root that is in the i/ü series, rather than the a/e series, which is the standard. These are:

almak	alır	to take/get
bulmak	bulur	to find
durmak	durur	to stop/to halt
kalmak	kalır	to remain/to stay
olmak	olur	to be/to become
sanmak	sanır	to suppose
varmak	varır	to arrive
vurmak	vurur	to strike/to hit
and		
bilmek	bilir	to know how to
gelmek	gelir	to come
görmek	görür	to see
ölmek	ölür	to die
vermek	verir	to give

The rich system of suffixes that are added at the end of verb stems to express tense, person and manner is remarkably regular and uniform in Turkish.

To express the English "have/has," one uses the word with its possessive ending, followed by the word **var** meaning "exists":

I have a car.	**Arabam var.**
	(literally, "my car exists")
He/She has a bicycle.	**Bisikleti var.**
	(literally, "his/her bicycle exists")

To say "don't/doesn't have" the word **yok** is used instead of **var**:

I don't have a ticket.	**Biletim yok.**
	(literally, "my ticket exists-not")
He/She doesn't have any money.	**Parası yok.**
	(literally, "his/her money exists-not")

Nouns and Articles

Nouns in Turkish change their ending according to their function in a sentence. These grammatical case endings are themselves subject to change due to vowel harmony. For beginners, it is often difficult to separate the case endings from the other suffixes added to a word and, therefore, it is better to learn words within a complete phrase.

Nouns do not have grammatical gender. The indefinite demonstrative article **bir** (literally, "one") corresponds closely to the English "a/an", however there is no definite article corresponding to the English "the". This article is generally conveyed by the demonstrative adjectives **bu/ şu** (this) and **o** (that).

Pronouns

The challenge for English speakers is to know when to use **sen** and **siz**, both of which are "you" in English. It is clear that a group of people must be addressed with **siz**, the second person plural pronoun. However, this same pronoun, like in some other languages, is used as a respectful form of address for unfamiliar, elderly or hierarchically higher individuals. For the tourist, it is safe to address the people one meets for the first time with **siz**, until familiarity develops or all agree to use the less formal **sen**. The latter form, **sen**, is the correct form to use among family members, good friends and with children.

I	**ben**
you (sing., inf.)	**sen**
he/she/it	**o**
we	**biz**
you (pl./form.)	**siz**
they	**onlar**

Word Order

Standard word order in Turkish is subject-object-verb. For instance:
Murat kedileri gördü.   Murat saw the cats.
Murat=subject, kedileri=object, gördü=verb.

Questions are formed either with question words:

ne   what
kim   who
nerede where
nasıl how
niçin why

Or, the question particle **mi** is appended after the word that is the focus of the question:

Murat kedileri gördü mü?	Did Murat *see* the cats?
Murat kedileri mi gördü?	Did Murat see the *cats*?
Murat mı kedileri gördü?	Was it *Murat* who saw the cats?

Negation

The letter **-m-**, added between the verb stem and what follows, indicates negation. Some examples:

He/She travels.	**Gezer.**	He/She does not travel.	**Gezmez.**
He/She is traveling.	**Geziyor.**	He/She is not traveling.	**Gezmiyor.**

Imperatives

The imperative for second person singular is simply the verbal stem. The negative imperative is the same with the **-m-** suffix.

Come! (one person)	**Gel!**
Don't come! (one person)	**Gelme!**

The positive and negative imperatives for second person plural or formal are the same pair, with the plural suffix:

Come! (several persons)	**Gelin!**
Don't come! (several persons)	**Gelmeyin!**

Comparative and Superlative

The comparative is generally formed with **daha** (more); it precedes the adjective. Example:

büyük	big
daha büyük	bigger

The preferred way for conveying the sense of "less" is again through the use of **daha** with the adjective that has the opposite meaning.

küçük	small
daha küçük	smaller

The superlative is formed by adding **en** in front of the adjective:

en büyük	the biggest
en küçük	the smallest

Adjectives

Adjectives come before the noun, and there are no case or singular/plural endings on them:

uzun yol	long road
uzun yollar	long roads
Uzun yoldan geldim.	I arrived from a long trip.
	(Literally: I arrived from a long road.)

Adverbs and Adverbial Expressions

Almost any adjective can be used as an adverb that modifies a verb:

güzel konuştu	he spoke beautifully
yavaş/süratli sürün!	Drive slowly/quickly!

Adverbs precede the verb or the adjective they qualify, and they take no case or singular/plural endings:

hızlı koşmak	to run fast
koyu mavi gözler	intensely blue eyes

Adverbs may be directional or time-related, or they may qualify the verb:

içeri	inside
ileri	forward
erken	early
geç	late
çok	a lot, too much
az	a little, too little

hemen	right away

The –ca/–ce suffix forms adverbs from adjectives or nouns:

sinsice	sneakily
kahramanca	heroically

Examples with some of the foregoing:

içeri girin!	Go inside!
çok yedim	I ate too much
erken gelin!	Come early!
sinsice yürüyor	he is walking sneakily
hemen yaparlar	They will do it right away

Numbers

0	**sıfır** sih·fihr
1	**bir** beer
2	**iki** ee·kee
3	**üç** yuch
4	**dört** durrt
5	**beş** behsh
6	**altı** ahl·tih
7	**yedi** yeh·dee
8	**sekiz** seh·keez
9	**dokuz** doh·kooz
10	**on** ohn
11	**on bir** ohn beer
12	**on iki** ohn ee·kee

13	**on üç** <u>ohn</u> yuch	
14	**on dört** <u>ohn</u> durrt	
15	**on beş** <u>ohn</u> besh	
16	**on altı** <u>ohn</u> ahl·<u>tih</u>	
17	**on yedi** <u>ohn</u> yeh·dee	
18	**on sekiz** <u>ohn</u> seh·<u>keez</u>	
19	**on dokuz** <u>ohn</u> doh·<u>kooz</u>	
20	**yirmi** yeer·<u>mee</u>	
21	**yirmi bir** yeer·<u>mee</u> <u>beer</u>	
22	**yirmi iki** yeer·<u>mee</u> ee·<u>kee</u>	
30	**otuz** oh·<u>tooz</u>	
31	**otuz bir** oh·tooz <u>beer</u>	
40	**kırk** kihrk	
50	**elli** ehl·<u>lee</u>	
60	**altmış** ahlt·<u>mihsh</u>	
70	**yetmiş** yeht·<u>meesh</u>	
80	**seksen** sehk·<u>sehn</u>	
90	**doksan** dohk·<u>sahn</u>	
100	**yüz** yyuz	
101	**yüz bir** yyuz <u>beer</u>	
200	**ikiyüz** ee·<u>kee</u> yyuz	
500	**beşyüz** <u>behsh</u> yyuz	
1,000	**bin** been	
10,000	**on bin** <u>ohn</u> been	
1,000,000	**bir milyon** <u>beer</u> meel·yohn	

Ordinal Numbers

first	**birinci**	bee·reen·<u>jee</u>
second	**ikinci**	ee·keen·<u>jee</u>
third	**üçüncü**	yu·chyun·<u>jyu</u>
fourth	**dördüncü**	durr·dyun·<u>jyu</u>
fifth	**beşinci**	beh·sheen·<u>jee</u>
once	**bir kere**	<u>beer</u> keh·reh
twice	**iki kere**	ee·<u>kee</u> keh·reh
three times	**üç kere**	<u>yuch</u> keh·reh

Time

Essential

What time is it?	**Saat kaç?** sah·<u>aht</u> <u>kahch</u>
It's noon [midday].	**Saat on iki.** sah·<u>aht</u> on ee·<u>kee</u>

At midnight.	**Gece yarısı.** geh·jeh yah·rih·sih
From nine o'clock to 5 o'clock.	**Saat dokuzdan beşe.** sah·<u>aht</u> doh·kooz·<u>dahn</u> beh·<u>sheh</u>
Twenty after [past] four.	**Dördü yirmi geçiyor.** durr·<u>dyu</u> yeer·<u>mee</u> geh·<u>chee</u>·yohr
A quarter to nine.	**Dokuza çeyrek var.** doh·koo·<u>zah</u> chay·<u>rehk</u> vahr
5:30 *a.m./p.m.*	**Öğleden *önce/sonra* beş buçuk.** ur·leh·<u>dehn</u> <u>urn</u>·jeh/*sohn*·rah behsh boo·<u>chook</u>

Days

Monday	**Pazartesi** pah·<u>zahr</u>·teh·see
Tuesday	**Salı** sah·<u>lih</u>
Wednesday	**Çarşamba** chahr·shahm·<u>bah</u>
Thursday	**Perşembe** pehr·shehm·<u>beh</u>
Friday	**Cuma** joo·<u>mah</u>
Saturday	**Cumartesi** joo·<u>mahr</u>·teh·see
Sunday	**Pazar** pa·<u>zar</u>

Dates

yesterday	**dün** dyun
today	**bugün** <u>boo</u>·gyun
tomorrow	**yarın** <u>yah</u>·rihn
day	**gün** gyun
week	**hafta** hahf·<u>tah</u>

172

| month | **ay** ie |
| year | **yıl** yihl |

Months

January	**Ocak** oh·jahk
February	**Şubat** shoo·baht
March	**Mart** mahrt
April	**Nisan** nee·sahn
May	**Mayıs** mah·yihs
June	**Haziran** hah·zee·rahn
July	**Temmuz** tehm·mooz
August	**Ağustos ah**·oos·tohs
September	**Eylül** ay·lyul
October	**Ekim** eh·keem
November	**Kasım** kah·sihm
December	**Aralık** ah·rah·lihk

Seasons

spring	**ilkbahar** eelk·bah·hahr
summer	**yaz** yahz
fall [autumn]	**sonbahar** sohn·bah·hahr
winter	**kış** kihsh

Holidays

January 1, New Year's Day	**Yılbaşı**
April 23, National Independence and Children's Day	**Ulusal Egemenlik ve Çocuk Bayramı**
May 19, Commemoration of Atatürk's Landing in Samsun and Youth and Sports Day	**Atatürk'ü Anma, Gençlik ve Spor Bayramı**
August 30, National Independence Victory Day	**Zafer Bayramı**
October 29, Republic Day	**Cumhuriyet Bayramı**

Movable Dates

Festival of Sweetmeats	**Şeker Bayramı**
Festival of Sacrifice	**Kurban Bayramı**

i April 23rd, National Sovereignty and Children's Day, is the anniversary of the opening of the Grand National Assembly, which happened in Ankara in 1920. Traditionally this is a holiday dedicated to children. May 19th, the Commemoration of Atatürk's Landing in Samsun, Youth and Sports Day, commemorates the start of the Turkish War of Independence, which began in 1919. Now this holiday is dedicated to youth and sports.

August 30th, Victory Day, memorializes the final victory that brought the War of Independence to an end in 1922. October 29th is the anniversary of the founding of the Turkish Republic in 1923.

The Festival of Sweetmeats and the Festival of Sacrifice are Muslim holidays whose dates are based on the lunar calendar, rather than the Gregorian calendar. The Festival of Sweetmeats is a three-holiday to mark the end of the month of Ramadan. The name marks the tradition of visiting friends and family with a gift of "sweetmeats."

The Festival of Sacrifice is a four-day holiday which commemorates the willingness of Abraham to sacrifice his son for Allah. It is celebrated by the sacrifice of an animal followed by a family feast and gifts of food to the poor.

Conversion Tables

Mileage

1 km – 0.62 mi	20 km – 12.4 mi
5 km – 3.10 mi	50 km – 31.0 mi
10 km – 6.20 mi	100 km – 61.0 mi

Measurement

1 gram	**gram** grahm	= 0.035 oz.
1 kilogram (kg)	**kilogram** kee·loh·grahm	= 2.2 lb
1 liter (l)	**litre** leet·reh	= 1.06 U.S./0.88 Brit. quarts
1 centimeter (cm)	**santimetre** sahn·tee·meht·reh	= 0.4 inch
1 meter (m)	**metre** meht·reh	= 3.28 feet
1 kilometer (km)	**kilometre** kee·loh·meht·reh	= 0.62 mile

Temperature

-40° C – -40° F	-1° C – 30° F	20° C – 68° F
-30° C – -22° F	0° C – 32° F	25° C – 77° F
-20° C – -4° F	5° C – 41° F	30° C – 86° F
-10° C – 14° F	10° C – 50° F	35° C – 95° F
-5° C – 23° F	15° C – 59° F	

Oven Temperature

100° C – 212° F	177° C – 350° F
121° C – 250° F	204° C – 400° F
149° C – 300° F	260° C – 500° F

Useful Websites

www.turizm.net
Turkey Travel Guide

www.gofethiye.com
Specialty site for Fethiye peninsula in Mugla province

www.tcdd.gov.tr/tcdding/index.htm
TCDD – Turkish State Railways

www.hihostels.com
Hostelling International website

www.tsa.gov
U.S. Transportation Security Administration (TSA)

www.ubak.gov.tr/ubak/en/index.php
Ministry of Transportation website

www.tourismturkey.org
Turkish Culture and Tourism website

www.gototurkey.co.uk
Turkish Culture and Tourism Office website

www.caa.co.uk
U.K. Civil Aviation Authority (CAA)

www.berlitzpublishing.com
Berlitz Publishing website

English–Turkish Dictionary

A

abroad yurtdışı
accept v kabul etmek
accident kaza
accompany v eşlik etmek
acetaminophen
  parasetamol
acne sivilce
adapter adaptör
address adres
after sonra
air conditioner klima
air sickness bag sıhhi
  torba
airmail uçak ile
airport havaalanı
aisle seat koridor kenarı
  koltuk
alarm clock çalar saat
all hepsi
allergy alerji
allow izin vermek

allowance (customs)
  gümrüksüz geçebilecek
  miktar
almost neredeyse
alone yalnız
already zaten
also ayrıca
alter v değiştirmek
alternate route alternatif
  yol
aluminum foil alimünyum
  kağıtı
always her zaman
amazing hayret verici
ambassador elçi
ambulance ambülans
American adj Amerikan;
  n Amerikalı
amount (money) tutar
amusement park oyun parkı
animal hayvan
another başka bir
antacid mide asidine karşı
  ilaç
antibiotics antibiyotik
antifreeze antifriz
antique (object) antika

antiseptic antiseptik

antiseptic cream antiseptik krem

anyone biri

apartment apartman dairesi

apologize v özür dilemek

appetite iştah

appointment randevu

April Nisan

area code alan kodu

arcade oyun salonu

around (place) yakınları; (time) civarında

arrival (terminal) variş

arrive v varmak

art gallery sanat galerisi

arthritis arterit

ask istemek

aspirin aspirin

assistance yardım

asthma astım

ATM paramatik

attack saldırı

attractive cazip

audio guide teybe alınmış rehber

August Ağustos

Australia Avustralya

authenticity hakikilik

automatic car otomatik araba

autumn [BE] sonbahar

B

baby bebek

baby bottle biberon

baby food bebek maması

baby wipes bebek mendili

babysitter çocuk bakıcısı

back (part of body) sırt

backpack sırt çanta

backache sırt ağrısı

bad kötü

bag çanta

baggage [BE] bavul

baggage cart alış veriş arabası

baggage check emanet

baggage claim bavul teslim bandi

baggage trolley [BE] alış veriş arabası

ball top

bandage bandaj

bank banka

bar bar

basket sepet

basketball basketbol

basketball game basketbol maçı

bathroom tuvalet

battery (vehicle) akü; (radio, watch) pil

battle site savaş meydanı

be v olmak

beach plaj

beautiful güzel

bed yatak

before önce

begin v başlamak

behind arkasında

belt kemer

bet n bahis

between (time) arasında

bicycle bisiklet

big büyük

bikini bikini

bill [BE] fatura; (receipt at restaurant) hesap

birthday doğum günü

bite (insect) sokmak

black siyah

blanket battaniye

blister su toplanması

blood pressure tansiyon

blouse bluz

blue mavi

boat trip tekne gezisi

book n kitap

book store kitapçı

boots bot; (sport) çizme

boring sıkıcı

botanical garden botanik bahçesi

bottle şişe

bottle opener şişe açacağı

box kutu

boxing match boks maçı

boy erkek çocuk

boyfriend erkek arkadaş

bra sütyen

break v kırmak

breast meme

breathe v nefes almak

bridge köprü

briefs külot

bring v getirmek

Britain Britanya

British Britanyalı

brooch broş

broom süpürge

bus otobüs

bus station otobüs garajı

bus stop otobüs durağı

business iş

business center iş merkezi

busy kalabalık

but ama

buy v satın almak

C

cable car teleferik
cafe kafe
calendar takvim
call v çağırmak;
  (telephone) aramak
call collect karşı tarafa
  ödetmek
camera fotoğraf makinesi
camp v kamp yapmak
campsite kamp alanı
can opener konserve
  açacağı
Canada Kanada
cancel v iptal etmek
car araba; (train
  compartment) vagon
car park [BE] otopark
car rental araba kiralama
car seat araba koltuğu
carafe sürahi
carpet (rug) halı
carry-on el çantası
carton kutu
cash para; nakit
cash desk [BE] kasa
cashier kasa

casino kumarhane
castle kale
cat kedi
catch v (bus) yetişmek
cathedral katedral
cave mağara
cell phone cep telefonu
certificate belge
change n (coins) bozuk
  para; v (alter) değiştirmek;
  (bus, train) aktarma
  yapmak; (money)
  bozdurmak
changing facilities bebeğin
  altını değiştirecek yer
charcoal odun kömürü
charge ücret
cheap ucuz
check fatura; (receipt at
  restaurant) hesap
check in v check-in
  yaptırmak
check-in desk uçuş kaydi
  masasi
check out (hotel) otelden
  ayrılmak
checking account cari
  hesap
chemist [BE] eczane
chest pain göğüs ağrısı

child çocuk
child seat çocuk
  sandalyesi
child's cot [BE] çocuk
  yatağı
church kilise
cigar puro
cigarette sigara
cinema [BE] sinema
classical music klasik
  müzik
clean adj temiz;
  v temizlemek
cleaning supplies temizlik
  maddeleri
clear silmek
cliff uçurum
cling film [BE] plastik
  ambalaj kağıdı
clock saat
close (near) yakın;
  v kapanmak
clothing store elbise
  mağazası
club (golf) sopa
coach (long-distance bus)
  şehirlerarası otobüs
coat palto
code (area) kod
coin madeni para

cold n (flu) soğuk algınlığı;
  adj (temperature) soğuk
colleague meslektaş
collect v almak
color renk
comb tarak
come v gelmek
commission komisyon
company (business)
  şirket; (companionship)
  arkadaşlık
computer bilgisayar
concert konser
concert hall konser salonu
conditioner saç kremi
condom prezervatif
conference konferans
confirm v teyit etmek
consulate konsolosluk
contact v bağlantı kurmak
contact lens kontak lens
contain v içermek
convention hall kongre
  salonu
cook ahçı
cooking facility pişirme
  olanağı; mutfak
copper bakır
corkscrew şarap açacağı
cost v tutmak

cot bebek yatağı
cotton (fabric) pamuklu;
  (cotton wool) pamuk
cough öksürük
country ülke
country code ülke kodu
courier (guide) rehber
cover charge masa ücreti
cramps kramp
credit card kredi kartı
crib çocuk yatağı
cruise n deniz yolculuğu
crystal (quartz) kuartz
cup fincan
currency para birimi
currency exchange office
  döviz bürosu
current account [BE] cari
  hesap
curtain perde
customs gümrük
cut kesik
cycling race bisiklet yarışı

D

damage n hasar
dance n dans; v dans
  etmek
dance club diskotek

dangerous curve tehlikeli
  kavşak
day gün
deaf sağır
December Aralık
deck chair katlanabilir
  koltuk
declare v beyan etmek
deep derin
delay gecikme
denim kot kumaşı
dentist diş doktoru
denture protez
deodorant deodoran
depart v (train, bus)
  kalkmak
department store mağaza
departure gate çıkış kapisi
deposit ön ödeme
desert çöl
detergent deterjan
diabetic (person) şeker
  hastası
diamond elmas
diaper bebek bezi
diarrhea ishal
dictionary sözlük
die ölmek
diesel dizel
difficult zor

directory (telephone) rehber
dirty kirli
disabled [BE] özürlü
discount indirim
dish (utensil) tabak çanak
dishwasher bulaşık makinesi
dishwashing liquid bulaşık deterjanı
disposable razor tek kullanımlık jilet
dive v dalmak
diving equipment dalış donanımı
divorced boşanmış
do v yapmak
doctor doktor
doll bebek
dollar (U.S.) dolar
domestic flight iç hat uçuşu
door kapı
double room çift kişilik oda
downtown area kent merkezi
dress elbise
dress code giyim tarzı
drive v seyretmek
driver sürücü

driver's license ehliyet
dry cleaner kuru temizleyici
duty gümrük vergisi
duty-free goods vergisiz eşyalar

E

earache kulak ağrısı
earrings küpe
east doğu
easy kolay
eat v yemek
economy class ekonomi sınıfı
eight sekiz
eighteen on sekiz
eighty seksen
electrical outlet elektrik prizi
electronic elektronik
elevator asansör
eleven on bir
e-mail n e-posta; v yazmak
e-mail address e-posta adresi
embassy elçilik
emergency acil durum
emergency exit acil çıkış
empty adj boş; v boşaltmak

end v bitmek
England İngiltere
English İngilizce
English-speaking İngilizce
konuşan
enjoy v beğenmek
enter v girmek
equipment (sports)
donanım
escalator yürüyen
merdiven
e-ticket e-bilet
e-ticket check-in e-bilet
kaydı
European Union AB
evening gece
excess luggage fazla bavul
ağırlığı
exchange v değiştirmek
exchange rate döviz kuru
excursion gezinti
exit n çıkış; v çıkmak
expensive pahalı
expert uzman
express ekspres
extension dahili hat
extra (additional) daha
extra bed ek yatak
eye göz

F

fabric kumaş
facial yüz bakımı
fall sonbahar
family aile
fan (ventilator) vantilatör
far uzak
farm çiftlik
far-sighted yakını görme
bozukluğu
fast (ahead) ileri;
(speed) hızlı
fast-food restaurant hazır
yemek lokantası
fax faks
February Şubat
fee komisyon
feed v yemek vermek
female kadın
ferry vapur
fever ateş
few birkaç tane
field tarla
fifteen on beş
fifty elli
fill v hazırlamak
fill up (car) doldurmak
filling (dental) dolgu
film film

find v bulmak
fine adj iyi
fire yangın
fire door yangın kapisi
fire extinguisher yangın
    söndürme aleti
first class birinci sınıf
fit v (clothes) olmak
fitting room soyunma odası
five beş
fix v onarmak
flat adj (shoe) patlak
flight uçuş
flight number uçuş
    numarası
floor (level) kat
fly v uçmak
folk music halk müziği
food yiyecek
football [BE] futbol
football game [BE] futbol
    maçı
foreign currency döviz
forest orman
fork çatal
form form
forty kırk
four dört
fourteen on dört
frame (glasses) çerçeve

free (available) boş;
    (without charge) ücretsiz
freezer dondurucu
fresh taze
Friday Cuma
friend arkadaş
full dolu

G

game (match) maç;
    (toy) oyun
garage (parking) garaj;
    (repair) araba
    tamirhanesi
garbage bag çöp torbası
garden bahçe
gas benzin
gas station benzin
    istasyonu
gate (airport) biniş kapısı
get v (find) bulmak
get a refund v para geri
    almak
get off v (bus, etc.) inmek
get to v gitmek
gift shop hediyelik eşya
    dükkanı
girl kız çocuk
girlfriend kız arkadaş

give *v* vermek
glass bardak
glasses (optical) gözlük
go *v* gitmek
gold altın
golf golf
golf club golf sopası
golf course golf sahası
golf tournament golf
  turnuvası
good *adj* iyi
green yeşil
grocery store bakkal
ground (earth) zemin
ground-floor room zemin-
  kat odası
guide (telephone) [BE]
  rehber; (tour) gezi rehberi
guide dog rehber köpeği
guide book rehber kitabı
gym jimnastik
gynecologist kadın
  hastalıkları uzmanı

H

hair saç
hairbrush saç fırçası
haircut saç tıraşı
hairdresser kuaför

hairspray saç spreyi
half *adj* yarım
hand el
handbag [BE] cüzdan
handicapped özürlü
happen *v* olmak
harbor liman
hard (difficult) zorlu;
  (solid) sert
hat şapka
have *v* sahip olmak
hear *v* duymak
heart kalp
heat *n* ısıtıcı
heater ısıtıcı
heating [BE] *n* ısıtıcı
heavy ağır
helmet kask
help yardım
here burada
high yüksek
highchair yüksek sandalye
highway otoyol
hill tepe
hire [BE] *v* kiralamak
hold on *v* (wait) beklemek
holiday [BE] tatil
home ev
horsetrack at yarışı
hospital hastane

hot sıcak
hotel otel
hour saat
house ev
how nasıl
hundred yüz
hungry aç
hurt v acımak
husband koca

I

ibuprofen ibuprofen
ice buz
identification kimlik
  belgesi
ill [BE] hasta
included dahil
incredible inanılmaz
indoor pool kapalı havuz
inexpensive ucuz
infection bulaşma
information bilgi
information desk danışma
  masası
information office danışma
  bürosu
innocent masum
insect böcek
insect bite böcek sokması

insect repellent böcek
  kovucu
inside içerde
instant messenger anında
  muhabbet
instruction kullanım
  talimatı
insurance sigorta
interest (hobby) ilgi alanı
interesting ilginç
intermediate orta seviyede
international flight diş hat
  uçuşu
internet internet
internet cafe internet kafe
internet service internet
  hizmeti
interpret tercüme etmek
interpreter tercüman
intersection kavşak
Ireland İrlanda
iron ütü
item eşya
itemized bill dökümlü
  hesap

J

jacket monta
January Ocak

jazz caz
jeans kot pantalon
jet-ski jet ski
jeweler kuyumcu
jewelry mücevherat
job iş
join v (accompany)
  katılmak; (to get involved)
  girmek
July Temmuz
June Haziran

K

key anahtar
key ring anahtarlık
kiddie pool çocuk havuzu
kilometer kilometre
kiss v öpmek
kitchen mutfak
kitchen foil [BE] alimünyum
  kağıtı
know v bilmek

L

lace dantel
lake göl
land v (airplane) inmek
large büyük

last adj son; sonuncu;
  v devam etmek
late geç
launderette [BE]
  çamaşırhane
laundromat çamaşırhane
laundry facility
  çamaşırhane
lawyer avukat
leather deri
leave v (depart) kalkmak;
  (deposit) bırakmak;
  (go) gitmek
left (side) sol
leg bacak
lens (camera) objektif;
  (glasses) cam
letter mektup
library kitaplık
life boat cankurtaran
  sandalı
life jacket can yeleği
lifeguard cankurtaran
lift [BE] asansör
lift pass teleferik pasosu
light n (electric) ışık;
  adj (not dark) aydınlık;
  (not heavy) hafif; (color)
  açık; (on vehicle) far
light bulb ampul

lighter (cigarette) çakmak
like *v* beğenmek
line (subway) hat
linen keten
liquor store tekel bayii
lira (Turkish currency, YTL) lira
liter litre
little (small) küçük
live *v* yaşamak
live music canlı müzik
local yerel
lock kilit
log on *v* girmek
login giriş
logout *n* çıkış; *v* çıkmak
long uzun
look like *v* benzemek
lose *v* kaybetmek
love *v* (like) beğenmek; (somebody) sevmek
low düşük
low bridge alçak köprü
luggage bavul
luggage cart el arabası
luggage locker bagaj dolapı

M

machine washable makinede yıkanabilir
magazine dergi
magnificent muhteşem
mail mektup
mailbox posta kutusu
main ana; başlıca
make-up *n* makyaj; *v* (a prescription) [BE] hazırlamak
male (man) erkek
mall alış veriş merkezi
manager müdür
manicure manikür
manual (car) el kitabı
map harita
March Mart
market pazar
mascara rimel
massage masaj
May Mayıs
match (smoking) kibrit; (sports) maç
measurement ölçü
medicine (medication) ilaç
medium (size) orta
meet *v* buluşmak
meeting toplantı

meeting room toplantı
  odası
message mesaj
microwave mikrodalga
midnight gece yarısı
mistake yanlışlık
mobile phone [BE] cep
  telefonu
moisturizer (cream)
  nemlendirici
moment an
Monday Pazartesi
money para
month ay
mop yer bezi
moped mopet
mosque cami
motion sickness yol
  tutması
motorboat motorlu tekne
motorcycle motorsiklet
motorway [BE] otoyol
mountain dağ
mouth ağız
move v taşınmak
movie film
movie theater sinema
movies theater sinema
mugging hırsızlık
museum müze

music müzik

N

nail file tırnak törpüsü
name isim
napkin peçete
nappy [BE] bebek bezi
national ulusal
near yakın
necklace kolye
new yeni
New Zealand Yeni Zelanda
newspaper gazete
newsstand gazete bayii
next (following) bir sonraki
next to yanında
nice iyi
nightclub gece klübü
nine dokuz
nineteen on dokuz
ninety doksan
non-smoking sigara
  içilmeyen
north kuzey
nose burun
nothing hiçbir şey
notify v bildirmek
November Kasım
novice acemi

number numara
nurse hemşire

O

October Ekim
office ofis
office hours çalışma
  saatleri
off-licence [BE] tekel bayii
off-peak kalabalık saatler
  dışında
often sık sık
old (senior) yaşlı;
  (thing) eski
one bir
one way tek yön
one-way ticket sırf gidiş
open adj açık; v (store)
  açılmak; v (a window)
  açmak
opening hours açılış
  saatleri
opera opera
opposite karşıda;
  karşısında
optician göz doktoru
orange (color) portakal
  rengi
order v sipariş vermek

outdoor açık havada
outdoor pool açık havuz
outside dışında; dışarda
overlook hakim tepe

P

pacifier emzik
pack v hazırlamak
package paket
paddling pool [BE] çocuk
  havuzu
pain acı
palace saray
pants pantalon
pantyhose tayt
paper towels kağıt havlusu
paracetamol [BE]
  parasetamol
park park
parking park yeri
parking lot otopark
party (social) parti
pass v (a place) geçmek
pass through geçmek
passport pasaport
passport control pasaport
  kontrolu
pastry store pastane
path patika

pay v ödemek
payment ödeme
peak tepe
pedestrian crossing yaya
 geçidi
pediatrician çocuk doktoru
people insanlar
period (menstrual) aybaşı
person kişi
petrol [BE] benzin
petrol station [BE] benzin
 istasyonu
pewter kurşun-kalay
 alaşımı
pharmacy eczane
phone n telefon; v telefon
 etmek
phone call telefon
 görüşmesi
phone card telefon kartı
photocopy fotokopi
photograph fotoğraf
phrase book konuşma
 kılavuzu
pick up v almak
picnic area piknik alanı
piece (item) parça
pill hap; (contraceptive)
 doğum kontrol hapı
pillow yastık

pillow case yastık kılıfı
PIN pin numarası
piste [BE] pist
place yer
plane uçak
plaster [BE] bandaj
plastic wrap plastik
 ambalaj kağıdı
plate tabak
platform [BE] peron
platinum platin
play n (theater) tiyatro
 oyunu; v (game) oynamak;
 (music) çalmak
playground çocuk parkı
plunger plançer
pocket cep
pole kayak sopası
point v (to something)
 göstermek
police polis
police report polis raporu
police station polis
 karakolu
pond gölcük
pop music pop
port (harbor) liman
post [BE] n posta; v postaya
 vermek
postbox [BE] posta kutusu

post office [BE] postane
postcard kartpostal
pottery çanak çömlek
pound (sterling) İngiliz
  sterlini
pregnant hamile
prescription reçete
press v ütülemek
price fiyat
problem soru
program program
purple mor
purpose sebeb
purse cüzdan
push chair [BE] puşet
put v koymak

Q

quarter çeyrek
quiet sessiz

R

racetrack hipodrom
racket (tennis, squash)
  raket
railway station [BE] tren
  garı
raincoat yağmurluk

rainy yağmurlu
rap rep
rape tecavüz
rash kaşıntı
razor jilet
razor blades jilet
ready hazır
real (genuine) gerçek;
  hakiki
receipt fatura; fiş
recommend v önermek
refrigerator buzdolabı
region bölge
regular (gas) normal;
  (size) orta boy
religion din
rent v kiralamak
repair v onarmak
repeat v tekrarlamak; tekrar
  etmek
report v (crime) haber
  vermek
reservation yer ayırtmak
reserve (a table)
  v ayırtmak
restaurant lokanta
restroom tuvalet

return (ticket) [BE] gidiş dönüş; v (come back) dönmek; (surrender) bırakmak
right (correct) doğru
ring yüzük
river ırmak
road yol
road map yol haritası
robbery soygun
romantic romantik
room oda
room service oda servisi
round (of game) tur
round-trip gidiş dönüş
route yol
rubbish [BE] çöp
rubbish bag [BE] çöp torbası

S

safe n kasa; adj (not dangerous) güvenli
sales tax KDV
sandals sandalet
sanitary napkin kadın bağı
sanitary pad [BE] kadın bağı
Saturday Cumartesi

sauna sauna
saving (account) tasarruf hesap
scarf eşarp
schedule tarife
scissors makas
Scotland İskoçya
sea deniz
seat (theater, movies) yer; (train) koltuk
see v görmek; (witness) tanık olmak
sell v satmak
seminar seminer
send göndermek
senior citizen yaşlı
separately ayrı ayrı
September Eylül
service (church) ayin; (to a customer) servis
seven yedi
seventeen on yedi
seventy yetmiş
shampoo şampuan
sheet (bed) çarşaf
ship gemi
shirt (men's) gömlek
shoe ayakkabı
shoe store ayakkabı dükkânı

shopping area alış veriş merkezi

shopping centre [BE] alış veriş merkezi

short kısa

shorts şort

show v göstermek

shower duş

side effect yan etkisi

sick hasta

sightseeing tour tur

silk ipek

silver gümüş

single (ticket) [BE] sırf gidiş

single room tek kişilik oda

sit v oturmak

six altı

sixteen on altı

sixty altmış

size beden

skirt etek

skis kayak

slippers terlik

slow (behind) geri; (speed) yavaş

small küçük

smoking sigara içilen

smoking area sigara içilen yer

sneakers lastik ayakkabı

snorkel şnorkel

snorkeling equipment şnorkel takımı

snow n kar; v kar yağmak

snowboard kar kayağı

snowshoe kar ayakkabısı

snowy karlı

soap sabun

soccer futbol

soccer game futbol maçı

sock çorap

socket priz

some bazı

something bir şey

soon yakında

soother [BE] emzik

sore throat boğaz ağrısı

south güney

souvenir hediyelik eşya

souvenir guide hediyelik eşya rehberi

souvenir store hediyelik eşya dükkanı

speak v konuşmak; (language) bilmek

special özel

sport spor

sports massage spor masajı

sprain burkulma
spring ilkbahar
square (town) meydan
stadium stadyum
stairs merdivenler
stamp n (postage) pul;
  v mühürletmek
start v (car) çalıştırmak;
  (commence) başlamak
stay v kalmak
steep dik
stomach mide
stomachache mide ağrısı
stop n (bus) durak;
  (subway) metro istasyonu;
  v durmak
store mağaza
store directory mağaza
  rehberi
store guide [BE] mağaza
  rehberi
stove fırın
straight ahead doğru
  ilerde
strange şaşırtıcı
stream dere
strike v (hit) vurmak
stroller puşet
student öğrenci
study v okumak

summer yaz
Sunday Pazar
suppose sanmak
style üslup
subway metro
subway map metro planı
subway station metro
  istasyonu
suggest v önermek
suit takım elbise
suitable uygun
sun güneş
sunburn güneş yanığı
sunglasses güneş gözlüğü
sunny güneşli
sunscreen güneş geçirmez
  krem
sunstroke güneş çarpması
super (petrol) [BE] süper
superb mükemmel
supermarket süpermarket
suppository fitil
surfboard surf tahtası
sweater süveter
sweatshirt sweatshirt
swelling şişlik
swim v yüzmek
swimming pool yüzme
  havuzu
swimming trunks mayo

English-Turkish Dictionary

swimsuit mayo
synagogue havra

T

table masa
tablet tablet
take v (carry) götürmek;
  (medicine) almak; (room)
  tutmak; (time) binmek
take off çıkartmak
talk v konuşmak
tampon tampon
taxi taksi
taxi stand taksi durağı
team takım
tell v söylemek
ten on
tennis court tenis kortu
tennis match tenis maçı
tent çadır
terminal terminal
terrible berbat; kötü
that o
theft hırsızlık
thermal spring termal
  kaynağı
thick kalın
thief hırsız
thin ince

thirteen on üç
thirty otuz
this bu
three üç
throat boğaz
Thursday Perşembe
ticket bilet
ticket office bilet gişesi
tie kravat
tights [BE] tayt
time saat
timetable [BE] tarife
tissue kağıt mendil
tobacconist tütüncü
today bugün
toilet [BE] tuvalet
toilet paper tuvalet kağıdı
tomorrow yarın
too (extreme) çok
too much çok fazla
tooth diş
toothache diş ağrısı
toothbrush diş fırçası
toothpaste diş macunu
tour (sightseeing) tur
tourist turist
tourist office turist danışma
  bürosu
towel havlu
town şehir; kent

town map kent haritası
town square kasaba
   meydanı
toy store oyuncakçı
track peron
traditional geleneksel
traffic light trafik ışığı
trail pist
trail map pist haritası
train tren
train station tren garı
trash çöp
travel agency seyahat
   acentası
travel sickness [BE] yol
   tutması
traveler's check seyahat
   çeki
traveller's cheque [BE]
   seyahat çeki
trim uçlarından alma
trip yolculuk; gezi
trousers [BE] pantalon
try on v (clothes) denemek
T-shirt tişört
Tuesday Salı
tunnel tünel
Turkey Türkiye
Turkish (language) Türkçe;
   (nationality) Türk

turn off v kapatmak
turn on v açmak
TV televizyon
twelve on iki
twenty yirmi
two iki
typical tipik

U

ugly çirkin
umbrella şemsiye
under altında
underground [BE] metro
underground map [BE]
   metro planı
underground station [BE]
   metro istasyonu
underpants [BE] külot
understand v anlamak
United Kingdom Birleşik
   Krallık
United States of America
   Amerika Birleşik
   Devletleri
unlimited mileage sınırsız
   yakıt kullanımı
until kadar
upset stomach mide
   bozukluğu

urgent acil
use v kullanmak

V

vacation tatil
vacation resort tatil yeri
vacuum cleaner elektrikli
 süpürge
vaginal infection vajina
 iltihabı
valley vadi
value değer
VAT [BE] KDV
vegetarian (meal) etsiz;
 (person) vejetaryen
very çok
village köy
vineyard bağ
visa vize
visit n ziyaret; v ziyaret
 etmek
visiting hours ziyaret
 saatleri
volleyball voleybol
volleyball game voleybol
 maçı
vomit v kusmak

W

wait v beklemek
waiter garson
waitress garson
wake (someone)
 uyandırmak
wake-up call
 arama·uyandirma
walking route yürüyüş yolu
wallet cüzdan
warm ılık
washing machine çamaşır
 makinesi
watch (wrist) kol saati
water su
water skis su kayağı
waterfall şelale
way yol
weather hava
weather forecast hava
 tahmini
Wednesday Çarşamba
weekend rate hafta sonu
 fiyatı
west batı
what ne
wheelchair tekerlekli
 sandalye

wheelchair ramp tekerlekli sandalye rampası
when ne zaman
where nerede
who kim
why niçin
wife karı
window (office, apartment) pencere
window case vitrin
window seat pencere kenarı koltuk
windsurfer rüzgar sörfçüsü
winery şaraphane
wireless internet kablosuz internet
winter kış
withdraw funds çekilen paralar
within (time) içinde
wool yün
work v (function) çalışmak
wrong yanlış

Y

yield yol vermek
youth hostel gençlik yurdu

Z

zero sıfır
zoo hayvanat bahçesi

Turkish–English Dictionary

A

AB European Union
acemi novice
acı pain
acımak hurt v
acil urgent
acil çikiş emergency exit
acil durum emergency
aç hungry
açık open adj; light adj (color)
açık havada outdoor
açık havuz outdoor pool
açılış saatleri opening hours
açılmak open v (store)
açmak open v (a window); turn on
adaptör adapter
adres address
ağır heavy
ağız mouth
Ağustos August
ahçı cook
aile family

aktarma yapmak change v (bus, train)
akü battery (vehicle)
alan kodu area code
alçak köprü low bridge
alış veriş arabası baggage cart [trolley BE]
alerji allergy
alış veriş merkezi mall [shopping centre BE]; shopping area
alimünyum kağıtı aluminum [kitchen BE] foil
almak collect v; pick up; take (medicine)
altı six
altın gold
altında under
alternatif yol alternate route
altmış sixty
ama but
ambülans ambulance
Amerika Birleşik Devletleri United States of America
Amerikalı American n
Amerikan American adj
ampul light bulb
an moment
ana main

anahtar key
anahtarlık key ring
anında muhabbet instant
  messenger
anlamak understand v
antibiyotik antibiotics
antifriz antifreeze
antika antique (object)
antiseptik antiseptic
antiseptik krem antiseptic
  cream
apartman dairesi
  apartment
araba car
araba kiralama car rental
araba koltuğu car seat
araba tamirhanesi garage
  (repair)
Aralık December
aramak call v (telephone)
arama-uyandirma wake-up
  call
arasında between (time)
arkadaş friend
arkadaşlık company
  (companionship)
arkasında behind
arterit arthritis
asansör elevator [lift BE]
aspirin aspirin

astım asthma
at yarışı horsetrack
ateş fever
avukat lawyer
Avustralya Australia
ay month
ayakkabı shoe
ayakkabı dükkânı shoe
  store
aybaşı period (menstrual)
aydınlık period adj
  (not dark)
ayırtmak reserve v (a table)
ayrı ayrı separately
ayrıca also
ayin service (church)

bacak leg
bagaj dolapı luggage
  locker
bağ vineyard
bağlantı kurmak contact v
bahçe garden
bahis bet n
bakır copper
bakkal grocery store
bandaj bandage
  [plaster BE]

banka bank
bar bar
bardak glass
basketbol basketball
basketbol maçı basketball
  game
başka bir another
başlamak begin v; start
  (commence)
başlıca main
batı west
battaniye blanket
bavul luggage [baggage BE]
bavul teslim bandi baggage
  claim
bazı some
bebeğin altını değiştirecek
  yer changing facilities
bebek baby; doll
bebek bezi diaper [nappy
  BE]
bebek maması baby food
bebek mendili baby wipes
bebek yatağı cot
beden size
beğenmek enjoy v; like v;
  love
beklemek hold on v; wait
belge certificate
benzemek look like v

benzin gas [petrol BE]
benzin istasyonu gas
  [petrol BE] station
berbat terrible
beş five
beyan etmek declare v
bırakmak return v
  (surrender); leave
  (deposit)
biberon baby bottle
bikini bikini
bildirmek notify v
bilet ticket
bilet gişesi ticket office
bilgi information
bilgisayar computer
bilmek know v; speak
  (language)
biniş kapısı gate (airport)
binmek take v (time)
bir one
bir şey something
bir sonraki next (following)
biri anyone
birinci sınıf first class
birkaç tane few
Birleşik Krallık United
  Kingdom
bisiklet bicycle
bisiklet yarışı cycling race

bitmek end v
bluz blouse
boğaz throat
boğaz ağrısı sore throat
boks maçı boxing match
boş free (available); empty
boşaltmak empty v
boşanmış divorced
bot boots
botanik bahçesi botanical
    garden
bozdurmak change v
    (money)
bozuk para change n
    (coins)
böcek insect
böcek kovucu insect
    repellent
böcek sokması insect bite
bölge region
Britanya Britain
Britanyalı British
broş brooch
bu this
bugün today
bulaşık deterjanı
    dishwashing liquid
bulaşık makinesi
    dishwasher
bulaşma infection

bulmak find v; get
buluşmak meet v
burada here
burkulma sprain
burun nose
buz ice
buzdolabı refrigerator
büyük big; large

C

cam glasses
cami mosque
can yeleği life jacket
cankurtaran lifeguard
cankurtaran sandalı life
    boat
canlı müzik live music
cari hesap checking
    [current BE] account
caz jazz
cazip attractive
cep pocket
cep telefonu cell [mobile
    BE] phone
check-in yaptırmak
    check in v
civarında around (time)
Cuma Friday
Cumartesi Saturday

cüzdan purse [handbag BE]; wallet

Ç

çadır tent
çağırmak call v
çakmak lighter (cigarette)
çalar saat alarm clock
çalışma saatleri office hours
çalışmak work v (function)
çalıştırmak start v (car)
çalmak play v (music)
çamaşır makinesi washing machine
çamaşirhane laundromat [launderette BE]; laundry facility
çanak çömlek pottery
çanta bag
çarşaf sheet (bed)
Çarşamba Wednesday
çatal fork
çekilen paralar withdraw funds
çerçeve frame (glasses)
çeyrek quarter
çıkartmak take off
çıkış exit n; logout

çıkış kapisi departure gate
çıkmak exit v; logout
çift kişilik oda double room
çiftlik farm
çirkin ugly
çizme boots (sport)
çocuk child
çocuk bakıcısı babysitter
çocuk doktoru pediatrician
çocuk havuzu kiddie [paddling BE] pool
çocuk parkı playground
çocuk sandalyesi child seat
çocuk yatağı crib [child's cot BE]
çok too (extreme); very
çok fazla too much
çorap sock
çöl desert
çöp trash [rubbish BE]
çöp torbası garbage [rubbish BE] bag

D

dağ mountain
daha extra (additional)
dahil included
dahili hat extension

dalış donanımı diving equipment

dalmak dive v

danışma bürosu information office

danışma masası information desk

dans dance n

dans etmek dance v

dantel lace

değer value

değiştirmek change v (alter); alter; exchange

denemek try on v (clothes)

deniz sea

deniz yolculuğu cruise n

deodoran deodorant

dere stream

dergi magazine

deri leather

derin deep

deterjan detergent

devam etmek last v

dışarda outside

dışında outside

dik steep

din religion

diş tooth

diş ağrısı toothache

diş doktoru dentist

diş fırçası toothbrush

diş hat uçuşu international flight

diş macunu toothpaste

diskotek dance club

dizel diesel

doğru right (correct)

doğru ilerde straight ahead

doğu east

doğum günü birthday

doğum kontrol hapı pill (contraceptive)

doksan ninety

doktor doctor

dokuz nine

dolar dollar (U.S.)

doldurmak fill up (car)

dolgu filling (dental)

dolu full

donanım equipment (sports)

dondurucu freezer

dökümlü hesap itemized bill

dönmek return v (come back)

dört four

döviz foreign currency

döviz bürosu currency exchange office

döviz kuru exchange rate
durak stop *n* (bus)
durmak stop *v*
duş shower
duymak hear *v*
düşük low

E

e-bilet e-ticket
e-bilet kaydı e-ticket
  check-in
eczane pharmacy
  [chemist BE]
ehliyet driver's license
ek yatak extra bed
Ekim October
ekonomi sınıfı economy
  class
ekspres express
el hand
el arabası luggage cart
  [trolley BE]
el çantası carry-on
el kitabı manual (car)
elbise dress
elbise mağazası clothing
  store
elçi ambassador
elçilik embassy

elektrik prizi electrical
  outlet
elektrikli süpürge vacuum
  cleaner
elektronik electronic
elli fifty
elmas diamond
emanet baggage check
emzik pacifier [soother BE]
e-posta e-mail *n*
e-posta adresi e-mail
  address
erkek male (man)
erkek arkadaş boyfriend
erkek çocuk boy
eski old (thing)
eşarp scarf
eşlik etmek accompany *v*
eşya item
etek skirt
etsiz vegetarian (meal)
ev home; house
Eylül September

F

faks fax
far light *adj* (on vehicle)
fatura receipt [bill BE]

fazla bavul ağırlığı excess luggage
fırın stove
film film; movie
fincan cup
fiş receipt
fitil suppository
fiyat price
form form
fotoğraf photograph
fotoğraf makinesi camera
fotokopi photocopy
futbol soccer [football BE]
futbol maçı soccer [football BE] game

G

garaj garage (parking)
garson waiter; waitress
gazete newspaper
gazete bayii newsstand
gece evening
gece klübü nightclub
gece yarısı midnight
gecikme delay
geç late
geçmek pass v (a place); pass through
geleneksel traditional

gelmek come v
gemi ship
gençlik yurdu youth hostel
gerçek real (genuine)
geri slow (behind)
getirmek bring v
gezi trip
gezi rehberi guide (tour)
gezinti excursion
gidiş dönüş round-trip [return BE] (ticket)
giriş login
girmek enter v; log on; join (to get involved); get to; go; leave (go)
giyim tarzı dress code
golf golf
golf sahası golf course
golf sopası golf club
golf turnuvası golf tournament
göğüs ağrısı chest pain
göl lake
gölcük pond
gömlek shirt (men's)
göndermek send v
görmek see v
göstermek point v (to something); show
götürmek take v (carry)

göz eye
göz doktoru optician
gözlük glasses (optical)
gümrük customs
gümrük vergisi duty
gümrüksüz geçebilecek miktar allowance (customs)
gümüş silver
gün day
güneş sun
güneş çarpması sunstroke
güneş geçirmez krem sunscreen
güneş gözlüğü sunglasses
güneş yanığı sunburn
güneşli sunny
güney south
güvenli safe *adj* (not dangerous)
güzel beautiful

H

haber vermek report *v* (crime)
hafif light *adj* (not heavy)
hafta sonu fiyatı weekend rate
hakiki real (genuine)

hakikilik authenticity
hakim tepe overlook
halı carpet (rug)
halk müziği folk music
hamile pregnant
hap pill
harita map
hasar damage *n*
hasta sick [ill BE]
hastane hospital
hat line (subway)
hava weather
hava tahmini weather forecast
havaalanı airport
havlu towel
havra synagogue
hayret verici amazing
hayvan animal
hayvanat bahçesi zoo
hazır ready
hazır yemek lokantası fast-food restaurant
hazırlamak fill [make-up BE] (a prescription) *v*; pack
Haziran June
hediyelik eşya souvenir
hediyelik eşya dükkanı gift shop; souvenir store

hediyelik eşya rehberi souvenir guide
hemşire nurse
hepsi all
her zaman always
hesap check (receipt at restaurant, etc.)
hırsız thief
hırsızlık mugging; theft
hızlı fast (speed)
hiçbir şey nothing
hipodrom racetrack

I

ılık warm
ırmak river
ısıtıcı heat *n*; heater [heating BE]
ışık light *n* (electric)

i

ibuprofen ibuprofen
iç hat uçuşu domestic flight
içerde inside
içermek contain *v*
içinde within (time)
iki two
ilaç medicine (medication)

ileri fast (ahead)
ilgi alanı interest (hobby)
ilginç interesting
ilkbahar spring
inanılmaz incredible
ince thin
indirim discount
İngiliz sterlini pound (sterling)
İngilizce English
İngilizce konuşan English-speaking
İngiltere England
inmek get off *v* (bus); land (airplane)
insanlar people
internet internet
internet hizmeti internet service
internet kafe internet cafe
ipek silk
iptal etmek cancel *v*
İrlanda Ireland
ishal diarrhea
isim name
İskoçya Scotland
istemek ask
iş business; job
iş merkezi business center
iştah appetite

iyi fine *adj*; good; nice
izin vermek allow

J

jet ski jet-ski
jilet razor; razor blades
jimnastik gym

K

kablosuz internet wireless
  internet
kabul etmek accept *v*
kadar until
kadın female
kadın bağı sanitary napkin
  [pad BE]
kadın hastalıkları uzmanı
  gynecologist
kafe cafe
kağıt havlusu paper towels
kağıt mendil tissue
kalabalık busy
kalabalık saatler dışında
  off-peak
kale castle
kalın thick
kalkmak depart *v* (train,
  bus); leave (depart)

kalmak stay *v*
kalp heart
kamp alanı campsite
kamp yapmak camp *v*
Kanada Canada
kapalı havuz indoor pool
kapanmak close *v*; turn off
kapı door
kar snow *n*
kar ayakkabısı snowshoe
kar kayağı snowboard
kar yağmak snow *v*
karı wife
karlı snowy
karşı tarafa ödetmek call
  collect
karşıda opposite
karşısında opposite
kartpostal postcard
kasa cashier [cash desk
  BE]; safe
kasaba meydanı town
  square
Kasım November
kask helmet
kaşıntı rash
kat floor (level)
katedral cathedral
katılmak join *v*
  (accompany)

katlanabilir koltuk deck chair

kavşak intersection

kayak skis

kayak sopası pole

kaybetmek lose v

kaza accident

KDV sales tax [VAT BE]

kedi cat

kemer belt

kent town

kent haritası town map

kent merkezi downtown area

kesik cut

keten linen

kırk forty

kırmak break v

kısa short

kış winter

kız arkadaş girlfriend

kız çocuk girl

kibrit match (smoking)

kilise church

kilit lock

kilometre kilometer

kim who

kimlik belgesi identification

kiralamak rent [hire BE] v

kirli dirty

kişi person

kitap book n

kitapçı bookstore

kitaplık library

klasik müzik classical music

klima air conditioner

koca husband

kod code (area)

kol saati watch (wrist)

kolay easy

koltuk seat (train)

kolye necklace

komisyon commission; fee

konferans conference

kongre salonu convention hall

konser concert

konser salonu concert hall

konserve açacağı can opener

konsolosluk consulate

kontak lens contact lens

konuşma kılavuzu phrase book

konuşmak talk v; speak

koridor kenarı koltuk aisle seat

kot kumaşı denim

kot pantolon jeans

koymak put *v*
köprü bridge
kötü terrible (weather); bad
köy village
kramp cramps
kravat tie
kredi kartı credit card
kuaför hairdresser
kuartz crystal (quartz)
kulak ağrısı earache
kullanım talimatı
  instruction
kullanmak use *v*
kumarhane casino
kumaş fabric
kurşun-kalay alaşımı
  pewter
kuru temizleyici dry cleaner
kusmak vomit *v*
kutu box; carton
kuyumcu jeweler
kuzey north
küçük little; small
külot briefs
  [underpants BE]
küpe earrings

L

lastik ayakkabı sneakers

liman harbor; port
lira (Turkish currency, YTL)
  lira
litre liter
lokanta restaurant

M

maç match (sports); game
  (match)
madeni para coin
mağara cave
mağaza store; department
  store
mağaza rehberi store
  directory [guide BE]
makas scissors
makinede yıkanabilir
  machine washable
makyaj make-up *n*
manikür manicure
Mart March
masa table
masa ücreti cover charge
masaj massage
masum innocent
mavi blue
Mayıs May
mayo swimming trunks;
  swimsuit

mektup letter; mail
meme breast
merdivenler stairs
mesaj message
meslektaş colleague
metro subway
 [underground BE]
metro istasyonu subway
 [underground] stop;
 subway [underground BE]
 station
metro planı subway
 [underground BE] map
meydan square (town)
mide stomach
mide ağrısı stomachache
mide asidine karşı ilaç
 antacid
mide bozukluğu upset
 stomach
mikrodalga microwave
monta jacket
mopet moped
mor purple
motorlu tekne motorboat
motorsiklet motorcycle
muhteşem magnificent
mutfak kitchen; cooking
 facility
mücevherat jewelry

müdür manager
mühürletmek stamp v
mükemmel superb
müze museum
müzik music

nakit cash n
nasıl how
ne what
ne zaman when
nefes almak breathe v
nemlendirici moisturizer
 (cream)
nerede where
neredeyse almost
niçin why
Nisan April
normal regular (gas)
numara number

o that
objektif lens (camera)
Ocak January
oda room
oda servisi room service
odun kömürü charcoal

ofis office
okumak study v
olmak be v; fit (clothes);
  happen
on ten
on altı sixteen
on beş fifteen
on bir eleven
on dokuz nineteen
on dört fourteen
on iki twelve
on sekiz eighteen
on üç thirteen
on yedi seventeen
onarmak fix v; repair
opera opera
orman forest
orta medium (size)
orta boy regular (size)
orta seviyede intermediate
otel hotel
otelden ayrılmak check out
  (hotel)
otobüs bus
otobüs durağı bus stop
otobüs garajı bus station
otomatik araba automatic
  car
otopark parking lot
  [car park BE]

otoyol highway
  [motorway BE]
oturmak sit v
otuz thirty
oynamak play v (game)
oyun game (toy)
oyun parkı amusement
  park
oyun salonu arcade
oyuncakçı toy store

Ö

ödeme payment
ödemek pay v
öğrenci student
öksürük cough
ölçü measurement
ölmek die
ön ödeme deposit
önce before
önermek recommend v;
  suggest
öpmek kiss v
özel special
özür dilemek apologize v
özürlü handicapped
  [disabled BE]

P

pahalı expensive
paket package
palto coat
pamuk cotton (cotton wool)
pamuklu cotton (fabric)
pantalon pants
  [trousers BE]
para cash *n*; money
para birimi currency
para geri almak get
  a refund *v*
paramatik ATM
parasetamol
  acetaminophen
  [paracetamol BE]
parça piece (item)
park park
park yeri parking
parti party (social)
pasaport passport
pasaport kontrolu passport
  control
pastane pastry store
patika path
patlak *adj* flat (shoe)
pazar market
Pazar Sunday
Pazartesi Monday

peçete napkin
pencere window (office,
  apartment)
pencere kenarı koltuk
  window seat
perde curtain
peron track [platform BE]
Perşembe Thursday
piknik alanı picnic area
pil battery (radio, watch)
pin numarasi PIN
pişirme olanağı cooking
  facility
pist trail [piste BE]
pist haritası trail map
plaj beach
plançer plunger
plastik ambalaj kağıdı
  plastic wrap [cling
  film BE]
platin platinum
polis police
polis karakolu police
  station
polis raporu police report
pop pop music
portakal rengi orange (color)
posta mail *n* [post BE]
posta kutusu mailbox
  [postbox BE]

postane post office
postaya vermek mail v
  [post BE]
prezervatif condom
priz socket
program program
protez denture
pul stamp n (postage)
puro cigar
puşet stroller [push
  chair BE]

raket racket (tennis,
  squash)
randevu appointment
reçete prescription
rehber courier (guide);
  directory [guide BE]
  (telephone)
rehber kitabı guide book
rehber köpeği guide dog
renk color
rep rap
rimel mascara
romantik romantic
rüzgar sörfçüsü windsurfer

saat clock; hour; time
sabun soap
saç hair
saç fırçası hairbrush
saç kremi conditioner
saç spreyi hairspray
saç tıraşı haircut
sağır deaf
sahip olmak have v
saldırı attack
Salı Tuesday
sanat galerisi art gallery
sandalet sandals
sanmak suppose
saray palace
satın almak buy v
satmak sell v
sauna sauna
savaş meydanı battle site
sebeb purpose
sekiz eight
seksen eighty
seminer seminar
sepet basket
sert hard (solid)
servis service (to customer)
sessiz quiet
sevmek love v (somebody)

seyahat acentası travel agency

seyahat çeki traveler's check [cheque BE]

seyretmek drive *v*

sıcak hot

sıfır zero

sıhhi torba air sickness bag

sık sık often

sıkıcı boring

sınırsız yakıt kullanımı unlimited mileage

sırf gidiş one-way [single BE] ticket

sırt back (part of body)

sırt ağrısı backache

sırt çanta backpack

sigara cigarette

sigara içilen smoking

sigara içilen yer smoking area

sigara içilmeyen non-smoking

sigorta insurance

silmek clear

sinema movie theater [cinema BE]

sipariş vermek order *v*

sivilce acne

siyah black

soğuk cold *adj* (temperature)

soğuk algınlığı cold *n* (flu)

sokmak bite (insect)

sol left (side)

son last *adj*

sonbahar fall [autumn BE]

sonra after

sonuncu last *adj*

sopa club (golf)

soru problem

soygun robbery

soyunma odası fitting room

söylemek tell *v*

sözlük dictionary

spor sport

spor masajı sports massage

stadyum stadium

su water

su kayağı water skis

su toplanması blister

surf tahtası surfboard

süper super (gas [petrol BE])

süpermarket supermarket

süpürge broom

sürahi carafe

sürücü driver
sütyen bra
süveter sweater
sweatshirt sweatshirt

Ş

şampuan shampoo
şapka hat
şarap açacağı corkscrew
şaraphane winery
şaşırtıcı strange
şehir town
şehirlerarası otobüs coach
  (long-distance bus)
şeker hastası diabetic
  (person)
şelale waterfall
şemsiye umbrella
şirket company (business)
şişe bottle
şişe açacağı bottle opener
şişlik swelling
şnorkel snorkel
şnorkel takımı snorkeling
  equipment
şort shorts
Şubat February

T

tabak plate
tabak çanak dish (utensil)
tablet tablet
takım team
takım elbise suit
taksi taxi
taksi durağı taxi stand
takvim calendar
tampon tampon
tanık olmak see v (witness)
tansiyon blood pressure
tarak comb
tarife schedule
  [timetable BE]
tarla field
tasarruf hesap saving
  (account)
taşınmak move v
tatil vacation [holiday BE]
tatil yeri vacation resort
tayt pantyhose [tights BE]
taze fresh
tecavüz rape
tehlikeli kavşak dangerous
  curve
tek kişilik oda single room
tek kullanımlık jilet
  disposable razor

tek yön one way
tekel bayii liquor store
  [off-licence BE]
tekerlekli sandalye
  wheelchair
tekerlekli sandalye rampası
  wheelchair ramp
tekne gezisi boat trip
tekrar etmek repeat v
tekrarlamak repeat v
teleferik cable car
teleferik pasosu lift pass
telefon phone n
telefon etmek phone v
telefon görüşmesi phone call
telefon kartı phone card
televizyon TV
temiz clean
temizlemek clean v
temizlik maddeleri cleaning
  supplies
Temmuz July
tenis kortu tennis court
tenis maçı tennis match
tepe hill; peak
tercüman interpreter
tercüme etmek interpret v
terlik slippers
termal kaynağı thermal
  spring

terminal terminal
teybe alınmış rehber audio
  guide
teyit etmek confirm v
tırnak törpüsü nail file
tipik typical
tişört T-shirt
tiyatro oyunu play n
  (theater)
top ball
toplantı meeting
toplantı odası meeting
  room
trafik ışığı traffic light
tren train
tren garı train [railway BE]
  station
tur round (of game);
  sightseeing tour
turist tourist
turist danışma bürosu
  tourist office
tutar amount (money)
tutmak take v (room); cost
tuvalet bathroom; restroom
  [toilet BE]
tuvalet kağıdı toilet paper
tünel tunnel
Türk Turkish (nationality)
Türkçe Turkish (language)

Türkiye Turkey
tütüncü tobacconist

U

ucuz cheap; inexpensive
uçak plane
uçak ile airmail
uçlarından alma trim
uçmak fly *v*
uçurum cliff
uçuş flight
uçuş kaydi masasi check-in
  desk
uçuş numarası flight
  number
ulusal national
uyandırmak wake
  (someone)
uygun suitable
uzak far
uzman expert
uzun long

Ü

ücret charge
ücretsiz free (without
  charge)
üç three

ülke country
ülke kodu country code
üslup style
ütü iron
ütülemek press *v*

V

vadi valley
vagon car (train
  compartment)
vajina iltihabı vaginal
  infection
vantilatör fan (ventilator)
vapur ferry
variş arrival (terminal)
varmak arrive *v*
vejetaryen vegetarian
  (person)
vergisiz eşyalar duty-free
  goods
vermek give *v*
vitrin window (store);
  window case
vize visa
voleybol volleyball
voleybol maçı volleyball
  game
vurmak strike *v* (hit)

yağmurlu rainy
yağmurluk raincoat
yakın near; close (near)
yakında soon
yakını görme bozukluğu
  far-sighted
yakınları around (place)
yalnız alone
yan etkisi side effect
yangın fire
yangin kapisi fire door
yangın söndürme aleti fire
  extinguisher
yanında next to
yanlış wrong
yanlışlık mistake
yapmak do v
yardım help; assistance
yarım half adj
yarın tomorrow
yaşamak live v
yaşlı senior citizen; old adj
  (senior)
yastık pillow
yastık kılıfı pillow case
yatak bed
yavaş slow (speed)

yaya geçidi pedestrian
  crossing
yaz summer
yazmak e-mail v
yedi seven
yemek eat v
yemek vermek feed v
yeni new
Yeni Zelanda New Zealand
yer place; seat (theater,
  movies)
yer ayırtmak reservation
yer bezi mop
yerel local
yeşil green
yetişmek catch v (bus)
yetmiş seventy
yirmi twenty
yiyecek food
yol road; route; way
yol haritası road map
yol tutması motion
  [travel BE] sickness
yol vermek yield
yolculuk trip
yurtdışı abroad
yüksek high
yüksek sandalye highchair
yün wool

yürüyen merdiven escalator

yürüyüş yolu walking route

yüz hundred

yüz bakımı facial

yüzme havuzu swimming pool

yüzmek swim *v*

yüzük ring

Z

zaten already

zemin ground (earth)

zemin-kat odası ground-floor room

ziyaret visit *n*

ziyaret etmek visit *v*

ziyaret saatleri visiting hours

zor difficult

zorlu hard (difficult)